A Note From Rick Renner

I am on a personal quest to see a "revival of the Bible" so people can establish their lives on a firm foundation that will stand strong and endure the test when the end-time storm winds begin to intensify.

In order to experience a revival of the Bible in your personal life, it is important to take time each day to read, receive, and apply its truths to your life. James tells us that if we will continue in the perfect law of liberty — refusing to be forgetful hearers but determined to be doers — we will be blessed in our ways. As you watch or listen to the programs in this series and work through this corresponding study guide, I trust that you will search the Scriptures and allow the Holy Spirit to help you hear something new from God's Word that applies specifically to your life. I encourage you to be a doer of the Word that He reveals to you. Whatever the cost, I assure you — it will be worth it.

> Thy words were found, and I did eat them;
> and thy word was unto me the joy and rejoicing of mine heart:
> for I am called by thy name, O Lord God of hosts.
> — Jeremiah 15:16

Your brother and friend in Jesus Christ,

Rick Renner

Unless otherwise indicated, all scripture quotations are taken from the *King James Version* of the Bible.

Scripture quotations marked (*AMPC*) are taken from the *Amplified® Bible*, Copyright © 1954, 1958, 1962, 1964, 1965, 1987 by The Lockman Foundation. Used by permission. **www.Lockman.org**.

Scripture quotations marked (*NKJV*) are taken from the *New King James Version*®. Copyright © 1982 by Thomas Nelson. Used by permission. All rights reserved.

Foundations of Faith

Copyright © 2019 by Rick Renner
8316 E. 73rd St.
Tulsa, Oklahoma 74133

Published by Rick Renner Ministries
www.renner.org

ISBN 13: 978-1-68031-616-2

eBook ISBN 13: 978-1-68031-654-4

All rights reserved. No portion of this book may be reproduced or transmitted in any form or by any means — electronic, mechanical, photocopy, recording, scanning, or other — except for brief quotations in critical reviews or articles, without the prior written permission of the Publisher.

How To Use This Study Guide

This ten-lesson study guide corresponds to *"Foundations of Faith" With Rick Renner* (**Renner TV**). Each lesson in this study guide covers a topic that is addressed during the program series, with questions and references supplied to draw you deeper into your own private study of the Scriptures on this subject.

To derive the most benefit from this study guide, consider the following:

First, watch or listen to the program prior to working through the corresponding lesson in this guide. (Programs can also be viewed at **renner.org** by clicking on the Media/Archives links.)

Second, take the time to look up the scriptures included in each lesson. Prayerfully consider their application to your own life.

Third, use a journal or notebook to make note of your answers to each lesson's Study Questions and Practical Application challenges.

Fourth, invest specific time in prayer and in the Word of God to consult with the Holy Spirit. Write down the scriptures or insights He reveals to you about being filled with the Spirit and empowered by Him in your daily life.

Finally, take action! Whatever the Lord tells you to do according to His Word, do it.

For added insights on this subject, it is recommended that you obtain Rick Renner's book

Promotion (Ten Guidelines To Help You Achieve Your Long-Awaited Promotion!) or other titles, including *Repentance* and *Sparkling Gems From the Greek, Volumes 1* and *2*. You may also select from Rick's other available resources by placing your order at **renner.org** or by calling 1-800-742-5593.

LESSON 1

TOPIC
Determining Your Spiritual Status

SCRIPTURES
1. **Hebrews 5:12-14** — For when for the time ye ought to be teachers, ye have need that one teach you again which be the first principles of the oracles of God; and are become such as have need of milk, and not of strong meat. For every one that useth milk is unskilful in the word of righteousness: for he is a babe. But strong meat belongeth to them that are of full age, even those who by reason of use have their senses exercised to discern good and evil.

GREEK WORDS
1. "ought" — ὀφείλω (*opheilo*): an obligation or necessity; something that should be achieved or accomplished; something that is owed; a moral duty
2. "teachers" — (*didaskaloi*): masterful teachers; those superior in their field of expertise; rabbis
3. "need" — (*chreia*): a deficit; a need that must be met
4. "principles" — (*stoicheion*): basic elements; fundamentals; rudimentary knowledge essential before advancing to higher education; foundational knowledge
5. "first" — (*arches*): first, beginning, or something that is elementary
6. "teach" — (*didasko*): systematic learning of a student through the ever-present instruction of a teacher
7. "milk" — (*gala*): milk; that which is given to infants or sucklings; baby food
8. "strong meat" — (*stereas trophes*): solid food; the food required for the maintenance of a healthy adult
9. "unskillful" — ϖ (*apeiros*): untested, undeveloped, unskillful, or inexperienced; insufficient knowledge that leads to failure due to ignorance

10. "babe" — ϖ (*nepios*): a baby; an infant; an uneducated, unenlightened child
11. "full age" — (*teleion*): mature; an adult with adult responsibilities
12. "exercised" — μ (*gumnadzo*): used to portray athletes who exercised, trained, and prepared for competition in the games of the ancient world; often translated "naked" because the removal of clothes was necessary to eliminate all hindrances that otherwise might impede the movements and progress of serious athletes
13. "discern" — (*diakrisis*): judgment; discernment

SYNOPSIS

In this ten-part study ***Foundations of Faith***, the following topics will be examined:

1. Determining Your Spiritual Status
2. Repentance: What It Is, What It Isn't, and How to Do It
3. What Is Saving Faith?
4. Three Types of Baptism in the New Testament
5. The Laying on of Hands
6. The Doctrine of Resurrection
7. The Doctrine of Eternal Judgment
8. A Transplant That Will Save Your Life
9. Are You Just a Listener or Are You a Disciple?
10. Understanding Your Spiritual Level

The emphasis of this lesson:

The Word of God provides a solid foundation of truth and strength that transcends time and generations. It is the platform upon which we can build our lives, our families, and our communities. But where there is an absence of Scripture, people lose the ability to discern right from wrong. With no firm grasp on basic doctrine, they forfeit robust faith and arrive at wrong spiritual conclusions. They believe things that sound good, but are not of God.

The ancient city of Ephesus was a place of great education and learning. It housed the third-largest library in the world at the beginning of the Second Century, the Celsus Library. Appropriately called "the light of Asia,"

Ephesus attracted people from all over the continent to study and learn in this city and in this unique facility.

Just a few steps from the library was the School of Tyrannus, the place where the apostle Paul taught the Word of God to countless people for more than two years. Paul knew the unparalleled value of God's Word in people's lives, and that is why he taught it every day, morning and evening, to whoever had a heart to hear and understand.

The Word provides us with a solid, sure foundation of truth and strength that transcends time and generations. It is the platform upon which we can best build our lives, our families, and our communities.

The Word of God Has Become the Missing Link in Many Churches

In many churches today, the rich teaching of Scripture is missing. Although there is amazing music, great motivational preaching, and inspirational teaching, there is a distinct absence of the verse-by-verse teaching of the Bible as the foundation for it all. When there is an absence of the teaching of Scripture, it creates an unstable environment for disastrous things to happen in the lives of God's people. They lose the ability to discern right from wrong and to make decisions about their lives based on godly wisdom. Now, more than ever, we need a revival of the Bible.

Just because a person grows older in years does not mean he or she matures spiritually. There are many believers today who have been saved and in church for years, yet they are biblically illiterate. Spiritually speaking, they should be in high school or beyond, but instead they remain stuck in first grade with no signs of preparedness for promotion or to be graduated to the next level spiritually.

To grow spiritually, we need to *hear* the Word and *apply* its wisdom. Maturity comes when we hear the truth and put it into practice.

Do you know where you are spiritually in your life? Do you need a personal revival of the Bible?

We Must Lay the Foundation Properly Before Building on It

The writer of Hebrews was concerned because believers were spiritually stuck in a place of immaturity. Hebrews 5:12 says, "For when for the time ye ought to be teachers, ye have need that one teach you again which be the first principles of the oracles of God; and are become such as have need of milk, and not of strong meat."

The word "ought" is the Greek word *opheilo*, which indicates *an obligation or necessity; something that should be achieved or accomplished; something that is owed;* or *a moral duty*. The word "teachers" is the Greek word *didaskaloi*, and it describes *a masterful teacher who is superior in his field of expertise*. It was the same word used to describe *rabbis* in the First Century. The writer of Hebrews was telling believers, "You have heard and seen a lot. You should already know these subjects at an expert level. You are obligated to teach others, yet you are unable to do so."

Why not? Hebrews 5:12 says, "…Ye have need that one teach you again…." The word "need" is the Greek word *chreia*, meaning *a deficit* or *a need that must be met*. In other words, these Hebrew believers had a real spiritual problem — they didn't know "the first principles of the oracles of God." The word "first" is from the Greek word *arches*, which describes *the beginning* or *something elementary*. "Principles" is the Greek word *stoicheion*, and it denotes *basic elements, fundamentals*, or *foundational or rudimentary knowledge essential before advancing to higher education*.

Those Hebrew believers, like many believers today, should have been experts in the things of God, and able to teach others. But they were not. Although they had heard the fundamentals of the faith, they didn't really know them and therefore couldn't advance to the next level. Without a firm grasp on the fundamentals — the primary principles of God's Word — people arrive at wrong spiritual conclusions, believing things that sound good, but are not scripturally correct.

These believers had heard and seen so much regarding the ABCs of the Christian faith that they should have been functioning on the level of a rabbi. Yet they needed someone to teach them the fundamentals all over again. The word "teach" in Hebrews 5:12 is from the Greek word *didasko*, and it denotes the *systematic learning of a student through the ever-present instruction of a teacher.* In other words, they needed the close, continual instruction and correction of a teacher — just like children in the first grade!

Immature Believers Can Only Handle Spiritual Milk

The writer of Hebrews continued by saying that these believers had "…become such as have need of milk, and not of strong meat." The word "milk" is from the Greek word *gala*, which indicates *milk given to infants or sucklings* or *baby food*. "Strong meat" is the Greek phrase *stereas trophes* and signifies *solid food* or *food required for the maintenance of a healthy adult*. Although these Hebrew converts had been saved for years, they were spiritually underdeveloped and could only handle spiritual baby food, not solid adult food.

Hebrews 5:13 says, "For every one that useth milk is unskilful in the word of righteousness: for he is a babe." Again, milk (*gala*) is used, along with "unskillful" — the Greek word *apeiros*, which means *untested, undeveloped, unskillful, or inexperienced* or *having insufficient knowledge, leading to failure due to ignorance.*

Essentially, those who eat only spiritual baby food are *untested, undeveloped,* and *inexperienced.* They can arrive at very illogical and erroneous conclusions regarding the fundamentals of the faith, perceiving things as *right* that are actually *wrong.*

Many believers today fall into this category. All they can handle is spiritual milk, not solid food. They're not growing in faith. They don't know the fundamental truths of the faith, and as a result they are confused as to what is right and wrong. They remain silent on issues like homosexuality, gender confusion, adultery, and fornication, etc. that destroy people's minds and emotions, families, and *lives.* And they do it primarily out of confusion or out of fear of being viewed as judgmental. Without the foundation of the Word of God, they are left "blowing in the wind" on many subjects (*see* Ephesians 4:14).

A person who lacks foundational knowledge of Scripture is called "a babe" (Hebrews 5:13). "Babe" is the Greek word *nipeos,* which describes *a baby, an infant,* or *an uneducated, unenlightened child.* Although we all start at this stage, we don't want to stay there. We should want to mature in our faith and move on to solid food.

Only Mature Believers Can Handle the 'Meat' of God's Word

Hebrews 5:14 goes on to say, "But strong meat belongeth to them that are of full age, even those who by reason of use have their senses exercised to discern good and evil." Here we see the phrase "strong meat" (*stereas trophes*), meaning *solid food for an adult's health*. This spiritual meat is reserved for those of "full age" — the Greek word *teleion*. This term denotes *a mature adult with adult responsibilities*. When a person graduates from spiritual *milk* to *solid food*, he has the nutrients he needs to think and act responsibly like an adult.

Scripture says these spiritually mature adults have had their senses "exercised," from the Greek word *gumnadzo*, a term used to portray *athletes who exercised, trained, and prepared for competition in the games of the ancient world*. It is often translated "naked" because the removal of clothes was often necessary to eliminate all hindrances that otherwise might have impeded the movements and progress of serious athletes.

This word "exercised" represents *serious spiritual commitment*. In other words, these are people who are willing to remove every hindrance from their life in order to ensure spiritual success.

When the Word of God is working in your heart and mind, you are "exercised" by it so you can come to a place spiritually where you're able to "discern good and evil" (Hebrews 5:14). The word "discern" is the Greek term *diakrisis*, and it means *to perceive, to discern*, or *to judge*. When the Word of God is working in you, it elevates you to a higher level in the Lord. You don't have to stop and say, "I wonder what God's will is in this situation?" You will have already discerned His will because you know His Word, and you have been "exercised" by it. You know how to act spiritually because you have grown into a spiritual adult.

STUDY QUESTIONS

Study to shew thyself approved unto God, a workman that needeth not to be ashamed, rightly dividing the word of truth.
— 2 Timothy 2:15

1. The Word of God is incomparable! There never has been, nor will there ever be, a book like it. Two passages to meditate on and hide in your heart are Second Timothy 3:16, 17 and Second Peter 1:20, 21. Take time to read these verses in two or three Bible translations. Then write out the version of each that impacts you most.
2. As you daily feed your spirit the Word of God, you can know with certainty that it is working inside you to transform you into the likeness of Christ. Read James 1:21, Hebrews 4:12, and Jeremiah 23:29. What do these promises, inspired by God's Spirit, declare that the Word is designed to do in you?

PRACTICAL APPLICATION

But be ye doers of the word, and not hearers only, deceiving your own selves.
—James 1:22

1. Be honest. If you were to evaluate your level of spiritual maturity, in what "grade" would you place yourself? Would you say first grade? Second grade? Sixth grade? College?
2. Are there some areas in your life in which you seem to be spiritually mature and other areas in which you can only handle "baby food"? You are not alone. Take a moment and make a brief list of areas where you feel spiritually mature and also areas where you feel you need to grow.
3. Turn to your Bible's concordance. Look up key words connected with the areas in which you feel you need to grow. Search the Scriptures for verses that deal with them. Write down any verse that really stands out to you. What is the Holy Spirit revealing to you through what you write?
4. Can you be spiritually mature in some area in a season of your life — and then *regress* in your level of maturity later? How we respond to the Word of God — esteeming it, giving attention to it, and applying it to our lives — determines how we fare in life as spiritual babies or adults or at some level in-between. Read Hebrews 2:1 and, using the principle you find there, write out your thoughtful answer to this question.

LESSON 2

TOPIC
Repentance: What It Is, What It Isn't, and How to Do It

SCRIPTURES

1. **Hebrews 5:12, 13** — For when for the time ye ought to be teachers, ye have need that one teach you again which be the first principles of the oracles of God; and are become such as have need of milk, and not of strong meat. For every one that useth milk is unskillful in the word of righteousness: for he is a babe.
2. **Hebrews 6:1, 2** — Therefore leaving the principles of the doctrine of Christ, let us go on unto perfection; not laying again the foundation of repentance from dead works, and of faith toward God, of the doctrine of baptisms, and of laying on of hands, and of resurrection of the dead, and of eternal judgment.
3. **Matthew 27:3** — Then Judas, which had betrayed him, when he saw that he was condemned, repented himself, and brought again the thirty pieces of silver to the chief priests and elders.
4. **Acts 17:30** — And the times of this ignorance God winked at; but now commandeth all men every where to repent.

GREEK WORDS

1. "ought" — (*opheilo*): an obligation or necessity; a moral duty
2. "teachers" — (*didaskaloi*): masterful teachers; those superior in their field of expertise; rabbis
3. "need" — (*chreia*): a deficit; a need that must be met
4. "first" — (*arches*): first, beginning, or something that is elementary
5. "principles" — (*stoicheion*): rudimentary knowledge essential before advancing to higher education; foundational knowledge
6. "unskillful" — ϖ (*apeiros*): untested, undeveloped, or inexperienced; insufficient knowledge that leads to failure due to ignorance

7. "first" — (*arches*): first, beginning, or something that is elementary
8. "go on" — (*phero*): to be carried along
9. "foundation" — μ (*themelios*): from μ (*tithimi*), to set or position, and (*lithos*), stone; something set in stone in our lives
10. "repentance" — μ (*metanoia*): a change of mind; a complete conversion; a turn, change of behavior, or new course; a completely altered view of life and behavior
11. "repented" — μ μ μ (*metamelomai*): profound sorrow; engulfed in grief; swallowed in regret

SYNOPSIS

The Celsus Library — the third-largest library in the world at the beginning of the Second Century — was built in about 110 A.D. in the heart of ancient Ephesus. Just adjacent to the Celsus was the School of Tyrannus and Philosopher's Square. It was at the School of Tyrannus where the apostle Paul taught the Word of God until the name of Jesus and the Scriptures themselves were heard by people from across Asia. Paul strongly believed people needed to be taught and established in the foundational doctrines of Christ and the Christian faith, including the doctrine of *repentance.*

The emphasis of this lesson:

Repentance entails a "turning" in one's thinking and believing toward God and His Word, and that change in thinking and believing results in a change of behavior. The proof that genuine repentance has taken place in a person is a marked change in his or her lifestyle.

Skilled in Fundamentals — the Key to Growth and Success

It's vital that every Christian knows what he or she believes. The book of Hebrews was written for that very purpose. The writer was very concerned that his readers didn't know the fundamental teachings of Scripture. He wrote, "…Ye ought to be teachers, [but] ye have need that one teach you again which be the first principles of the oracles of God…" (Hebrews 5:12). The word "ought" is from the Greek word *opheilo*, which describes *an obligation or necessity, a moral duty.* The word "teachers" is the Greek word *didaskaloi*, which portrays masterful teachers who were superior in their field of expertise — even on the level of rabbis.

In effect, the writer of Hebrews said, "With all the messages you've heard and the miracles you've seen, you should be highly skilled, expert teachers in the field of the fundamentals of the Christian faith. In fact, you have an obligation to teach others, but instead you need someone to teach you again."

Many of the Hebrew believers at that time had a deficit or lack of understanding of the "first principles (*stoicheion*) of the oracles of God." That is, they did not grasp *the rudimentary knowledge that was required to advance to the next level spiritually.*

The same is true for many believers today. We have to be established in the fundamentals of our faith before we can move on to more profound truth.

The Six Foundational Doctrines of the Faith

Continuing with the same theme, the writer of Hebrews went on to say, "Therefore leaving the principles of the doctrine of Christ, let us go on unto perfection; not laying again the foundation of repentance from dead works, and of faith toward God, of the doctrine of baptisms, and of laying on of hands, and of resurrection of the dead, and of eternal judgment" (Hebrews 6:1, 2).

Here again is the word "principles," from the Greek word *arches*, meaning *first, beginning*, or *something that is elementary*. It refers to the starting place of our faith in Christ. Then it says, "Let us go on unto perfection."

"Go on" is from the Greek word *phero*, which means *to be carried along*. This signifies God's desire that we not get stuck in spiritual "first grade," but that we fully grasp the fundamentals of the Christian faith and move on to deeper truths.

The writer then gives us the ABCs of the Christian faith that are essential for every believer:

- Repentance from dead works
- Faith toward God
- The doctrine of baptisms
- Laying on of hands

- Resurrection of the dead
- Eternal judgment

What about "the foundation of repentance from dead works"? The first thing we're to know and understand as believers is the foundation of *repentance*. We cannot be saved without the act of repentance — of turning completely to Christ.

The second fundamental doctrine is *faith toward God*, which is faith that is rooted in Christ and Christ alone. Third is *the doctrine of baptisms*, as there is more than one baptism in the New Testament.

Fourth is the *laying on of hands*, which is central to the faith. Next is the *resurrection of the dead*, which is at the very heart of our faith, followed by the doctrine of *eternal judgment*. In addition to the Great White Throne Judgment for unbelievers, there is also the Judgment Seat of Christ for all believers. We will each stand before Jesus and give an account for what we've done in this life — even with our life in Christ.

The Doctrine of Repentance

The "foundation of repentance from dead works" is the first doctrine listed in Hebrews 6:1. The word "foundation" is the Greek word *themelios*, and it means *to set something in stone in our lives*. The principle of repentance should be something set in stone in our lives.

"Repentance" is the Greek word *metanoia*, which means *a change of mind; a complete conversion; a turn, change of behavior, or new course; a completely altered view of life and behavior*.

Interestingly, there is absolutely no hint of emotion in the word *metanoia*. It can occur with emotion, but emotion is not required to repent. It implies a strictly intellectual decision. This change of thinking and believing results in a change of behavior. In other words, the proof that genuine repentance has taken place is a marked change in one's lifestyle.

Not everything that looks like repentance is actually true repentance. Judas Iscariot is an example of someone whose emotions may have indicated repentance, but Judas' actions after he betrayed the Lord were not those of true repentance.

The Scripture says in Matthew 27:3, "Then Judas, which had betrayed him, when he saw that he was condemned, repented himself, and brought again the thirty pieces of silver to the chief priests and elders." The word "repented" in this verse is the Greek word *metamelomai*, and it indicates *profound sorrow* and pictures someone *engulfed in grief* or *swallowed in regret*. Unlike *metanoia*, *metamelomai* is a completely emotional word. It has nothing to do with making a decision for Christ or changing the way one thinks. It indicates *regret*, not a change of heart, attitude, and behavior.

Jesus began His ministry calling people to *repentance* (*see* Matthew 4:17). When the apostle Peter preached on the Day of Pentecost, he told the people they needed to *repent* (see Acts 2:38). Repentance is the "birth canal" through which people must pass to enter the Kingdom of God. God "commandeth all men every where to repent" (Acts 17:30). This is His requirement — it is a decision of the mind, and no emotions are necessarily involved or required.

STUDY QUESTIONS

Study to shew thyself approved unto God, a workman that needeth not to be ashamed, rightly dividing the word of truth.
— 2 Timothy 2:15

1. Having wisdom and knowledge is extremely valuable and important. It is promised to you and me and to every believer who seeks to walk in one specific virtue — a virtue in which Jesus Himself delighted (*see* Isaiah 11:2, 3). Read Psalm 111:10, Proverbs 1:7, and Psalm 9:10 and identify this attribute that is bestowed upon you by the Holy Spirit as you abide in a relationship with Him.

2. In light of your answer to the previous question, what is one of the greatest confirmations that you are walking in this virtue? What specific actions should you be taking? Check out Psalm 34:11-14 and First Peter 3:8-12 for the answer.

3. What is the difference between the doctrine of repentance (*metanoia*) mentioned in Hebrews 6:1 and Judas' repentance (*metamelomai*) for his actions against Jesus recorded in Matthew 27:3? What characteristic indicates true repentance?

PRACTICAL APPLICATION

> But be ye doers of the word, and not hearers only, deceiving your own selves.
> —James 1:22

1. The Bible talks about six foundation doctrines: repentance from dead works; faith toward God; the doctrine of baptisms; laying on of hands; resurrection of the dead; and eternal judgment. In your own words, briefly describe what you know about each of these. If there is one or more you are unfamiliar with, it's okay. That is the purpose for this series.

2. According to Second Corinthians 7:10, there is both *worldly* sorrow and *godly* sorrow: "For godly grief and the pain God is permitted to direct, produce a repentance that leads and contributes to salvation and deliverance from evil, and it never brings regret; but worldly grief (the hopeless sorrow that is characteristic of the pagan world) is deadly [breeding and ending in death]" (*AMPC*). Describe the difference between worldly sorrow and godly sorrow. Share an example from your life in which God permitted godly sorrow to work in you — and you yielded to it — and what resulted because of it.

LESSON 3

TOPIC

What Is Saving Faith?

SCRIPTURES

1. **Hebrews 6:1, 2** — Therefore leaving the principles of the doctrine of Christ, let us go on unto perfection; not laying again the foundation of repentance from dead works, and of faith toward God, of the doctrine of baptisms, and of laying on of hands, and of resurrection of the dead, and of eternal judgment.

2. **Psalm 58:3** — The wicked are estranged from the womb: they go astray as soon as they be born, speaking lies.

3. **Romans 5:12** — Wherefore, as by one man sin entered into the world, and death by sin; and so death passed upon all men, for that all have sinned.
4. **Romans 3:23** — For all have sinned, and come short of the glory of God.
5. **Romans 5:8** — But God commendeth his love toward us, in that, while we were yet sinners, Christ died for us.
6. **2 Corinthians 5:17** — Therefore if any man be in Christ, he is a new creature: old things are passed away; behold, all things are become new.

GREEK WORDS
1. "foundation" — μ (*themelios*): from μ (*tithemi*), to set or position, and (*lithos*), stone; something set in stone in our lives
2. "repentance" — μ (*metanoia*): a change of mind; a decision to completely alter one's life and behavior
3. "first" — (*arches*): first, beginning, or something that is elementary
4. "faith toward God" — ϖ ϖ (*pisteos epi theon*): it is the picture of complete trust; it depicts no self-reliance; a faith that rests ONLY on God

SYNOPSIS
In the heart of the city of Ephesus was the renowned School of Tyrannus that is mentioned in Acts 19:9 and 10. It was housed in a building located close to the synagogue and was used as a school or lecture hall. Initially, the apostle Paul taught in the synagogue, but when he left the synagogue due to resistance, he moved into the School of Tyrannus where he taught every day for two years. He was so effective in his efforts that "…all they which dwelt in Asia heard the word of the Lord Jesus, both Jews and Greeks" (Acts 19:10).

The emphasis of this lesson:

God wants us to grow and move on to the deeper truths of the faith. But before we can move on to deeper truths, we must first understand and be established in the basics, which affect everything else in our lives. "Faith toward God" is one of those basic, foundational truths. In

fact, the only way to be saved, reconciled to God, and spend in eternity in Heaven is to have faith toward God — to trust in the sacrifice of Jesus Christ and His resurrection from the dead. Through faith in His righteous blood alone are we made right with God. Understanding this truth is foundational to our Christian life.

Faith's Foundations

You need to know what you believe as a Christian and to be established on the strong foundation of the fundamentals of the Christian faith. Hebrews 6:1 says, "Therefore leaving the principles of the doctrine of Christ, let us go on unto perfection...."

The word "leaving" means, in effect, *let's go on*, indicating God's desire for us to grow and move on to the deeper truths of the faith. But before we can move on to the *deeper truths*, we must first understand and be established in the *basics*, which affect everything else in our lives. These are listed in Hebrews 6:1 and 2: "...the foundation of repentance from dead works, and of faith toward God, of the doctrine of baptisms, and of laying on of hands, and of resurrection of the dead, and of eternal judgment."

The first foundational doctrine is the "foundation of repentance from dead works." The word "foundation" is from the Greek word *themelios*, and it means *to set something in stone*. The principle of repentance should be something set in stone in our lives — something permanently etched deeply in our hearts. "Repentance" is the Greek word *metanoia*, which means *a change of mind; a complete conversion; a turn, change of behavior, or new course; a completely altered view of life and behavior*.

As long as we're walking with the Lord, there will be issues we will need to deal with and to change — to turn around and *repent* of. As we saw in the last lesson, the Greek word for repentance in Hebrews 6:1 (*metanoia*) makes no suggestion of repentance as an emotional act. Repentance is a decision of the will that actually begins your Christian life.

In fact, without the act of repentance, we cannot be saved. It is the "birth canal" through which we must pass in order to enter the Kingdom of God. And repentance — the decision of the will to turn from a behavior or course — continues throughout our Christian walk.

'Faith Toward God' — the Second Foundation of the Faith

The Hebrew believers needed to be taught again "the first principles of the oracles of God" (Hebrews 5:12). The word "first" is the Greek term *arches*, which means *first, beginning,* or *something that is elementary*. God wanted the Hebrew Christians (and it is true for us today) to leave the starting point — the ABCs of the doctrines of Christ — and "go on unto perfection."

"Perfection" is the Greek word *teleiotes*, and it describes *a student who graduates from one class and moves on to the next one*. It describes the process of education and promotion.

In review, the *first* fundamental doctrine is that of "repentance from dead works." The *second* fundamental doctrine is "faith toward God" (*see* Hebrews 6:1). The Hebrew believers were struggling to put their faith solely in God and not also in their circumcision, the Law, temple sacrifices, taxes, and the traditions and culture of Judaism. They were trusting in a multitude of religious works to help make them right with God.

The phrase "faith toward God" is translated from three Greek words — *pisteos epi theon*, which describes a faith that is leaning on God and trusting wholly in Him. It is *the picture of complete trust*. It depicts *no self-reliance but, instead, a faith that rests only on God*.

It is good and right to do good works, especially things that will benefit others. In fact, good works are a sign that we are saved (*see* James 2:17, 18). However, our good deeds and behaviors do not in any way *earn* us our salvation. The only way to be saved and spend in eternity in Heaven is to trust in the sacrifice of Jesus Christ and His resurrection from the dead. It is through faith in His righteous blood alone that we are made right with God. If we are trusting in anything other than Christ, we are in eternal trouble.

It is impossible for us to save ourselves. We were each born a sinner — we possessed a sinful nature at birth (*see* Romans 5:12; Psalm 58:3). Romans 3:23 says, "For all have sinned, and come short of the glory of God."

Thankfully, God did not leave us in that condition. Instead, "God commendeth his love toward us, in that, while we were yet sinners, Christ died for us" (Romans 5:8). Those who embrace Christ's sacrifice are reborn —

changed: "Therefore if any man be in Christ, he is a new creature: old things are passed away; behold, all things are become new" (2 Corinthians 5:17).

Jesus' blood was the price paid for our redemption. Through faith in Him and His sacrifice *alone* are we saved. Understanding this truth is foundational to our Christian life.

STUDY QUESTIONS

> **Study to shew thyself approved unto God, a workman that needeth not to be ashamed, rightly dividing the word of truth.**
> **— 2 Timothy 2:15**

1. Carefully read Ephesians 2:8 and 9; Titus 3:4 and 5; and Romans 3:20-30. What is the Holy Spirit speaking to you through these passages about your faith toward God and being made righteous in the sight of God?
2. What gives you the authority to enter the presence of God? Check out these verses and write what the Holy Spirit reveals to you about your *access* into His presence: Hebrews 4:16; Hebrews 10:19-23; John 10:7-9; John 14:6; Ephesians 2:18; Ephesians 3:12.
3. Are you struggling to believe and accept what Christ has done for you through His death, burial, and resurrection? He wants you to stop struggling and learn to *rest* in Him. Take some time to read and meditate on Hebrews 3:12-19 and Hebrews 4:1-11 and explain what *your part* is in entering God's rest. How do these verses encourage you?

PRACTICAL APPLICATION

> **But be ye doers of the word, and not hearers only, deceiving your own selves.**
> **— James 1:22**

1. Be honest. If you died today and went to Heaven, on what basis should God grant you entrance?
2. Although we may not be trusting in things like circumcision, temple sacrifices, and paying temple taxes in order to be made right with God, we do sometimes trust in other things to try to ensure our right-standing with God. Stop and think about it. Are you putting

your confidence (faith) in something you're doing or not doing in order to be approved and accepted by God? If so, what is it?
3. Why do you think people struggle to believe they're saved? How does repeatedly hearing the question, "Are you *really* saved" work to produce doubt and fear? In your own words explain what it means — and what it looks like — to trust in Christ and *Christ alone* for your salvation.

LESSON 4

TOPIC
Three Types of Baptisms in the New Testament

SCRIPTURES

1. **Hebrews 6:1, 2** — Therefore leaving the principles of the doctrine of Christ, let us go on unto perfection; not laying again the foundation of repentance from dead works, and of faith toward God, of the doctrine of baptisms, and of laying on of hands, and of resurrection of the dead, and of eternal judgment.
2. **First Corinthians 12:13** — For by one Spirit are we all baptized into one body, whether we be Jews or Gentiles, whether we be bond or free; and have been all made to drink into one Spirit.
3. **Ephesians 4:4, 5** — There is one body, and one Spirit, even as yea re called in one hope of your calling; one Lord, one faith, one baptism.
4. **Galatians 3:27** — For as many of you as have been baptized into Christ have put on Christ.
5. **Matthew 3:11** — I indeed baptize you with water unto repentance: but he that cometh after me is mightier than I, whose shoes I am not worthy to bear: he shall baptize you with the Holy Ghost, and with fire.

GREEK WORDS

1. "first" — (*arches*): first, beginning, or something that is elementary
2. "baptisms" — ϖ μ (*baptismos*): to wash; to dip; to be fully immersed *into* something; to dip and dye; infers that there must be a baptizer, and there must be a medium into which a person is baptized

SYNOPSIS

The apostle Paul spent two years at the School of Tyrannus in Ephesus, preaching Christ and teaching the Word of God. Within that span of time, "all they which dwelt in Asia heard the word of the Lord Jesus, both Jews and Greeks" (Acts 19:10). It was to the Ephesians that Paul wrote a letter, which we have come to know as the book of Ephesians. It contains some of the deepest theological concepts in the entire New Testament. The Ephesian believers understood what Paul was saying because he had effectively taught them for two years. He had established them on the solid foundation of God's Word, causing them to be mentally and spiritually advanced.

In the same way, God wants us to be firmly established on the solid foundation of His Word. He wants us to know and understand what the Bible teaches — beginning with the six foundational doctrines outlined in Hebrews 6:1 and 2. These include the foundation of *repentance from dead works, faith toward God, the doctrine of baptisms, the laying on of hands, the resurrection of the dead*, and *the doctrine of eternal judgment*.

The emphasis of this lesson:

There are three different kinds of baptism in the New Testament. The first baptism is performed by the Holy Spirit, the second is performed by Jesus, and the third is performed by believers. The book of Acts is not just a history book, but a pattern book, providing us with a model of what the Church is and what it is called to do. In this book of patterns are examples of all three of these baptisms — the baptism into Christ, the baptism in the Holy Spirit, and water baptism.

God Wants You to Know the Fundamentals and Continue to Grow

Most believers want to go higher in their knowledge of God, which is a healthy, normal desire. However, before we can go higher and build solid, stalwart spiritual lives, we must first understand the foundational principles of the faith. Whatever is built on a faulty foundation is destined to tilt and perhaps totter and fall. Without a firm grasp of these fundamentals, we will make wrong moral decisions and make light of sinful behavior and its dangers in our own lives and the lives of others. On the contrary, with a solid understanding of the basics, we will have the stable platform we need to live well and to succeed in life.

In review of our previous lessons, we see that the Hebrew believers needed to be taught once again "the first principles of the oracles of God" (Hebrews 5:12). "First" is the Greek word *arches*, which describes the *first, beginning,* or *starting place* — and in this context, it describes the fundamentals of the Christian faith.

Three verses later in Hebrews 6:1, the writer said, "Therefore leaving the principles of the doctrine of Christ, let us go on unto perfection…." The word "perfection" is from *teleiotes* in the Greek, and it describes *a student who graduates from one level and moves on to the next.* This is God's intention for each of us — not to get stuck at any level spiritually, but to continually grow more and more into the image and likeness of Christ.

The Doctrine of Baptisms

The *third* foundational doctrine listed in Hebrews 6:1 and 2 is the *doctrine of baptisms*. The word "baptisms" is plural because there are three different kinds of baptism in the New Testament. The first baptism is performed by the Holy Spirit, the second is performed by Jesus, and the third is performed by believers.

The word "baptisms" is the Greek word *baptismos*, meaning *to wash, to dip,* or *to be fully immersed by someone into something.* This indicates that *there must be a baptizer and there must be a medium into which a person is baptized.* Interestingly, the oldest use of this word described taking a garment or cloth, dipping it into a vat of dye, and leaving it in the dye long enough to saturate that garment with the new color. When the person removed the material from the dye, it was totally changed from what it looked like previously.

This provides an excellent illustration of what happens to us when we first come to Christ and are saved. We are spiritually "dipped" into the blood of Jesus and completely cleansed of our sins. As we are saturated in the Blood, our spirit is totally changed and we are not like we were before we got saved. This is a picture of what happens at the *first baptism* — the baptism into Christ performed by the Holy Spirit.

The **first baptism** is performed by the *Holy Spirit* at salvation, and it does not require your participation. The moment you called on the name of the Lord and repented of your sin, the Holy Spirit supernaturally immersed you into the Body of Christ — the Church. Paul referred to this in First Corinthians 12:13, saying, "For by one Spirit are we all baptized into one body...." And in Galatians 3:27, he said, "For as many of you as have been baptized into Christ have put on Christ." This first baptism comes with salvation and is called the *baptism by the Spirit into the Body of Christ*. This baptism is alluded to in Ephesians 4:5, where it says, "One Lord, one faith, one baptism."

The **second baptism** is performed by *Jesus*, and it is referred to by many as the baptism in the Holy Spirit. In Matthew 3:11, John the Baptist said, "I indeed baptize you with water unto repentance: but he that cometh after me is mightier than I, whose shoes I am not worthy to bear: he shall baptize you with the Holy Ghost, and with fire." By definition, there must be a baptizer and a medium or "habitat" into which a person is baptized. Here, Jesus is the Baptizer, and the Holy Spirit is the medium into which a person is baptized.

The second baptism is also mentioned by Jesus in Luke 24:49 and Acts 1:5. It is what took place on the Day of Pentecost. Believers who were saved, having already experienced the first baptism into the Body of Christ, were baptized by Jesus into the Holy Spirit and began to speak in other tongues (*see* Acts 2:4). The second baptism is *not* required for salvation. That is, you do not have to speak in tongues to be saved. However, it is the second baptism that immerses you into the power of the Holy Spirit and enables you to experience and to be a conduit of the supernatural power of God.

The Second Baptism Is Visible Throughout the Book of Acts

Although a number of believers in the Church today view the second baptism as optional, the Early Church did not. In fact, throughout the book of Acts, you will see that once a person was saved, he was always led to the second baptism. This pattern is seen in Acts chapters 2, 8, 9, 10, and 19.

In Acts 2:4, we see the disciples of Jesus gathered and praying, obediently waiting for the "promise of the Father" as Jesus had instructed. Ten days after His ascension into Heaven, Jesus baptized all the disciples into the Holy Spirit. They were all filled with power and spoke in other tongues.

In Acts 8, we see that Philip went down to Samaria and preached Christ to the people. When the rest of the disciples heard that many of the Samaritans had been saved (experienced the first baptism into the Body of Christ), they sent Peter and John to pray and lay hands on them to receive the second baptism into the Holy Spirit. Acts 8:17 says, "…And they received the Holy Ghost."

In Acts 9, the apostle Paul (previously known as Saul) was miraculously saved on the road to Damascus. After being blinded by the light of Christ's presence, he was led by the hand into the city where he was prayed for by Ananias, a disciple of Christ. Paul not only received his sight, but also received this second baptism, the baptism into the Holy Spirit.

Then in Acts 10, we find Peter at the home of the devout Roman centurion Cornelius. As Peter shared the Gospel, in obedience to God after experiencing a vision by the power of the Holy Spirit (Acts 10:10-20), Cornelius and his entire household believed on the Lord Jesus and were instantly saved. Immediately after acting on their "faith toward God" for salvation and being baptized into Christ, they were also baptized by Jesus into the Holy Spirit and began to speak in tongues (*see* verses 44-46).

Then in Acts 19, approximately 23 years after the day of Pentecost, it is recorded that the apostle Paul arrived in Ephesus and met a group of disciples of John the Baptist. After sharing with them who Jesus was, they were saved — baptized into the Body of Christ. Paul then laid his hands on them for Jesus to baptize them in the Holy Spirit. Verse 6 states, "…The Holy Ghost came on them; and they spake with tongues, and prophesied."

The book of Acts is not just a history book, but a pattern book, providing us a model of what the Church is and what it is called to do. It shows that when people were baptized by the Holy Spirit into the Body of Christ (the first baptism), they were then baptized by Jesus into the Holy Spirit (the second baptism).

Believers also experienced the *third* baptism — the baptism in water.

The Third Baptism Is Also Vital to Living a Healthy Christian Life

The **third baptism** is performed by *other believers* and is called water baptism. Here, the baptizer is another believer, and the medium is water. This baptism can occur any time after salvation. It outwardly symbolizes, usually publicly, people's decision to bury their old life along with the "burial" that occurred in their new birth when they were baptized into Christ and their old nature was replaced with a new one as they became a new creature in Christ (*see* 2 Corinthians 5:17). This old lifestyle was an outward reflection of their old, sinful, unregenerate nature — it included their old ways of thinking, speaking, and acting.

Paul dedicated Romans chapter 6 entirely to this baptism. Although water baptism is not essential for salvation, it was a commandment given to every new believer by Jesus. This baptism — along with the first and second baptisms — is foundational to living a healthy Christian life. Believers who choose not to be water-baptized tend to struggle with obeying God throughout their lives.

As with the second baptism, throughout the book of Acts, there is a pattern of believers being saved and then water baptized. The Samaritans believed in Christ and were baptized (*see* Acts 8:12). Simon the Sorcerer believed and was baptized (*see* Acts 8:13). The eunuch whom Philip ministered to was also baptized (*see* Acts 8:13, 36, 38). After declaring Jesus as Lord, the apostle Paul was water baptized (*see* Acts 9:18). And Cornelius and his entire household were baptized immediately after being saved (*see* Act 10:47). The Bible also tells us the Philippian jailer and his household were all baptized after putting their faith in Christ (*see* Acts 16:33).

Clearly, the Early Church considered water baptism vital to being a disciple of Christ.

These three baptisms comprise the "doctrine of baptisms": The *first baptism* is the baptism into the Body of Christ and is done by the Holy Spirit. The *second baptism* is the baptism into the Holy Spirit and is performed by Jesus. The *third baptism* is the baptism into water and is conducted by believers. It is the will of God for you to experience all three of these baptisms.

STUDY QUESTIONS

Study to shew thyself approved unto God, a workman that needeth not to be ashamed, rightly dividing the word of truth.
— 2 Timothy 2:15

1. The first, second, and third baptisms are clearly visible throughout the book of Acts. Give a quick definition of each — identifying the *baptizer*, the *medium* into which one is baptized, and when that baptism should take place.
2. Of the three baptisms, which one is *mandatory* in order to go to Heaven? Which are not required for salvation, but if you choose not to receive them, your ability to obey the God's Word and walk in His power will be hindered?
3. Have you personally experienced each of these three baptisms? If so, briefly share your memory of each.

PRACTICAL APPLICATION

But be ye doers of the word, and not hearers only, deceiving your own selves.
— James 1:22

1. Rick explained the Greek word *baptismos* means *to wash, to dip*, or *to be fully immersed by someone into something*. It depicts dipping a garment or cloth into a vat of dye and leaving it in long enough to saturate it. In your own words, share how this illustration compares to your baptism into Jesus Christ, which takes place at salvation.
2. There are a number of believers today who view the second and third baptisms as optional. Why do you think this is so? Do you believe these two baptisms are optional? Briefly explain your answer.
3. God wants you to experience all three of these baptisms — including the second baptism, the baptism into the Holy Spirit. If Jesus has

never baptized you in the Holy Spirit, why not ask Him to do this right now? Simply reach out to Him in prayer and say, "Lord, baptize me in the power of Your Holy Spirit." If you prefer to have prayer help, you can call our ministry during office hours, and we will pray with you to experience this second baptism (1-800-RICK-593/ 1-800-742-5593). For additional encouragement, read Luke 11:9-13.

LESSON 5

TOPIC
The Laying on of Hands

SCRIPTURES
1. **Hebrews 5:12-14** — For when for the time ye ought to be teachers, ye have need that one teach you again which be the first principles of the oracles of God; and are become such as have need of milk, and not of strong meat.
2. **Hebrews 6:1, 2** — Therefore leaving the principles of the doctrine of Christ, let us go on unto perfection; not laying again the foundation of repentance from dead works, and of faith toward God, of the doctrine of baptisms, and of laying on of hands, and of resurrection of the dead, and of eternal judgment.
3. **Numbers 27:18** — And the Lord said unto Moses, Take thee Joshua the son of Nun, a man in whom is the spirit, and lay thine hand upon him.
4. **Deuteronomy 34:9** — And Joshua the son of Nun was full of the spirit of wisdom; for Moses had laid his hands upon him: and the children of Israel hearkened unto him, and did as the Lord commanded Moses.
5. **Mark 6:5** — And he could there do no mighty work, save that he laid his hands upon a few sick folk, and healed them.
6. **Luke 4:40** — Now when the sun was setting, all they that had any sick with divers diseases brought them unto him; and he laid his hands on every one of them, and healed them.
7. **Acts 6:5, 6** — ...They chose Stephen, a man full of faith and of the Holy Ghost, and Philip, and Prochorus, and Nicanor, and Timon,

rection of the dead, and *the doctrine of eternal judgment*. So far, we've covered repentance, faith toward God, and the doctrine of baptisms.

The *fourth* fundamental doctrine of the faith is the *laying on of hands*.

Human hands were designed by God to be instruments through which His gifts, authority, power, and blessing are to be imparted and transmitted from one person to another. This is well established in both the Old and New Testaments. Also, again and again, Scripture records that "the hand of the Lord" came on someone, infusing him with supernatural abilities and power to do the extraordinary.

Old Testament Examples of the Laying on of Hands

The first time the laying on of hands is seen most vividly is in Genesis 27 when Isaac passed on his blessing to his son Jacob. Isaac's hands served as the channel through which the blessing on his life would pass into the life of Jacob. Years later, Jacob wanted to pass the blessing he had received from Isaac into the lives of his grandsons. He carefully laid his hands on Ephraim and Manasseh, Joseph's sons, and imparted the blessing on them (*see* Genesis 48:14-16).

In Exodus 28 and 29, we find that Aaron and his sons were set apart to minister to the Lord as priests. After they were outfitted in fine linen garments and sacrifices were made, Moses laid his hands on them, anointing them with oil. He not only acknowledged the divine call of God on their lives, he also awakened it through the laying on of hands. They received divine impartations to serve God in the tabernacle as His priests.

In a similar way, before Moses died, he laid hands on Joshua and imparted divine authority and ability to lead the people of Israel into the Promised Land. Numbers 27:18 says, "And the Lord said unto Moses, Take thee Joshua the son of Nun, a man in whom is the spirit, and *lay thine hand upon him*." Deuteronomy 34:9 confirms the transfer that took place: "Joshua the son of Nun was full of the spirit of wisdom; for Moses had *laid his hands upon him*: and the children of Israel hearkened unto him, and did as the Lord commanded Moses."

The examples continue as the hand of the Lord came upon Ehud, Gideon, Jephthah, and Sampson to deliver Israel from her enemies and to serve as judges. Similarly, the hand of the Lord came on Saul and then David to serve as kings and lead the people. And then there was the mighty prophet of God Elijah. The hand of the Lord came upon him and empowered him to outrun King Ahab's chariot (*see* 1 Kings 18:46). This avenue of divine impartation continued right into the New Testament era.

Jesus Understood the Power of the Laying on of Hands

Beginning in Matthew's gospel, we see amazing examples of the laying on of hands in Jesus' ministry. In Matthew 8:3, Jesus put His hands on a man with leprosy, and he was cleansed. In verse 15, Jesus laid His hands on Peter's mother-in-law and healed her of a fever. In Matthew 9:29, Jesus laid His hands on the eyes of two blind men, and they received their sight. In Matthew 17:7, Jesus laid His hands on Peter, James, and John and imparted freedom from fear. Again in Matthew 20:34, Jesus laid hands on the eyes of two blind men and restored their sight.

In Mark 1:41, Jesus laid His hands on a leper, and power was released to cleanse him. In Mark 6:5, Jesus was in His hometown of Nazareth. Although He was ready and willing to do great things among the people, "He could there do no mighty work, save that *he laid his hands upon a few sick folk*, and healed them." Again in Mark 8:22-25, divine power was released through Jesus as He laid hands on a blind man from Bethsaida, restoring his sight.

Luke 4:40 says, "Now when the sun was setting, all they that had any sick with divers diseases brought them unto him; and *he laid his hands on every one of them*, and healed them." Anyone who was sick in the entire town, regardless of what disease he or she had, was brought before Jesus. He laid His hands on every single person, and when He did, healing power transferred through His hands into the people.

This only scratches the surface of all the miracles that took place through Jesus as He laid hands on people. The pattern continues into the book of Acts. Early believers understood that there was a "power transmission" that took place when they laid hands on people in the name of Jesus.

Early Believers Understood the Power of the Laying on of Hands

In Acts 6:5 and 6, the Bible says, "…They chose Stephen, a man full of faith and of the Holy Ghost, and Philip, and Prochorus, and Nicanor, and

Timon, and Parmenas, and Nicolas a proselyte of Antioch: whom they set before the apostles: and when they had prayed, *they laid their hands on them.*" Early believers knew that in order for these seven men to be empowered to serve in the ministry, they needed to lay their hands on them and impart God's power. It was not enough to just select them or just pray for them. They needed to lay their hands on them to impart God's power.

In Acts 8, after the Samaritans received the Word of God, the apostles in Jerusalem sent Peter and John to Samaria "…that they might receive the Holy Ghost" (v. 15). Verse 17 says, "Then *laid their hands on them,* and they received the Holy Ghost." The impartation of power was so visibly incredible that Simon the sorcerer offered Peter and John money for them to give him the same ability (*see* vv. 18, 19). They rejected Simon's offer and told him to repent of trying to buy God's power with money.

Then in Acts 9, we find Saul at a home on Straight Street in the city of Damascus. He had just had an encounter with Jesus. After having fasted for three days and having been without sight, he was visited by Ananias, a disciple of Christ. Immediately upon entering the house, Ananias *laid his hands on him* and prayed. Saul's eyes were opened and he was filled with the Holy Ghost (*see* vv. 17, 18).

In Acts 13 we see the ordination of Paul and Barnabas. Verses 2 and 3 reveal, "As they ministered to the Lord, and fasted, the Holy Ghost said, Separate me Barnabas and Saul for the work whereunto I have called them. And when they had fasted and prayed, and *laid their hands* on them, they sent them away." Through the laying on of hands, there was a transfer of the divine calling along with the anointing, gifting, and authority to carry it out.

A few years passed, and in Acts 19, Paul was entering the city of Ephesus where he found a group of disciples of John the Baptist. After sharing the Gospel and informing them about Christ, "…they were baptized in the name of the Lord Jesus. And when Paul had *laid his hands upon them,* the Holy Ghost came on them; and they spake with tongues, and prophesied" (vv. 5, 6). Paul knew that in addition to preaching the Gospel, he needed to lay his hands on them to impart the power of the Spirit.

We Must Practice the Laying on of Hands!

In First Timothy 4:14, Paul said to Timothy *and to us,* "Neglect not the gift that is in thee, which was given thee by prophecy, with the *laying on of the hands* of the presbytery." And in Second Timothy 1:6, Paul said, "...I put thee in remembrance that thou stir up the gift of God, which is in thee by the *putting on of my hands.*"

From the beginning of Scripture to the end, the doctrine of the laying on of hands is visibly demonstrated. Just before Jesus left the earth, He left us with this promise: "And these signs shall follow them that believe; In my name shall they cast out devils; they shall speak with new tongues; they shall take up serpents; and if they drink any deadly thing, it shall not hurt them: *they shall lay hands on the sick*, and they shall recover" (Mark 16:17, 18).

What can you do to see more miracles and demonstrations of God's power? Put into practice the doctrine of the laying on of hands. Your hands were designed by God to impart divine power, anointing, and blessing on others. Use it for His glory!

STUDY QUESTIONS

> Study to shew thyself approved unto God, a workman that needeth not to be ashamed, rightly dividing the word of truth.
> — 2 Timothy 2:15

1. Carefully reread the key verses related to the laying on of hands presented in the scripture section. What verse or passage stands out to you most? Why is it personally so impactful?

2. After reading through the verses, name as many blessings (gifts, benefits) as you can that are specifically imparted through the laying on of hands. In light of these blessings and the principle of Romans 2:11 and Romans 10:12, what certain truth can you take away? (*See* also Acts 10:34; Ephesians 6:9; and Job 34:18 for this recurring principle.)

PRACTICAL APPLICATION

> But be ye doers of the word, and not hearers only, deceiving your own selves.
> — James 1:22

1. As you can see from this lesson, the *laying on of hands* doctrine is demonstrated throughout both the Old and New Testaments. What was your understanding of this foundational truth *before* going through this lesson? How is your perspective different *after* the study?
2. First Timothy 4:14 says, "Neglect not the gift that is in thee, which was given thee by prophecy, with the laying on of the hands of the presbytery." Have you put into practice the laying on of hands? If so, how has the Holy Spirit blessed others through *your* hands? If you have neglected or shied away from the laying on of hands, why?
3. We see in Genesis 27 that Isaac laid his hands on his son Jacob and blessed him, and then Jacob did likewise with his grandsons Ephraim and Manasseh (*see* Genesis 48:14-16). Jesus also gave us this example by laying His hands on little children and blessing them (*see* Matthew 19:15 and Mark 10:16). Have you ever laid your hands on your children or grandchildren and prayed a blessing into their lives? If so, briefly describe what happened and what you prayed. If you haven't, take time to lay your hands on them and transfer a blessing on them.

LESSON 6

TOPIC
The Doctrine of the Resurrection

SCRIPTURES

1. **Hebrews 6:1, 2** — Therefore leaving the principles of the doctrine of Christ, let us go on unto perfection; not laying again the foundation of repentance from dead works, and of faith toward God, of the doctrine of baptisms, and of laying on of hands, and of resurrection of the dead, and of eternal judgment.
2. **John 11:25** — Jesus said unto her, I am the resurrection, and the life: he that believeth in me, though he were dead, yet shall he live.
3. **1 Corinthians 15:19, 20** — If in this life only we have hope in Christ, we are of all men most miserable. But now is Christ risen from the dead, and become the firstfruits of them that slept.
4. **1 Corinthians 15:3, 4** — For I delivered unto you first of all that which I also received, how that Christ died for our sins according to

the scriptures; and that he was buried, and that he rose again the third day according to the scriptures.

5. **Acts 1:3** — To whom also he shewed himself alive after his passion by many infallible proofs, being seen of them forty days, and speaking of the things pertaining to the kingdom of God.

6. **John 5:29** — And shall come forth; they that have done good, unto the resurrection of life; and they that have done evil, unto the resurrection of damnation.

7. **1 Thessalonians 4:15-18** — For this we say unto you by the word of the Lord, that we which are alive and remain unto the coming of the Lord shall not prevent them which are asleep. For the Lord himself shall descend from heaven with a shout, with the voice of the archangel, and with the trump of God: and the dead in Christ shall rise first: then we which are alive and remain shall be caught up together with them in the clouds, to meet the Lord in the air: and so shall we ever be with the Lord. Wherefore comfort one another with these words.

8. **1 Corinthians 15:51-53** — Behold, I shew you a mystery; we shall not all sleep, but we shall all be changed, in a moment, in the twinkling of an eye, at the last trump: for the trumpet shall sound, and the dead shall be raised incorruptible, and we shall be changed. For this corruptible must put on incorruption, and this mortal must put on immortality.

9. **Philippians 3:20, 21 (*NKJV*)** — For our citizenship is in heaven, from which we also eagerly wait for the Savior, the Lord Jesus Christ, who will transform our lowly body that it may be conformed to His glorious body, according to the working by which He is able even to subdue all things to Himself.

10. **Revelation 20:4, 5** — And I saw thrones, and they sat upon them, and judgment was given unto them: and I saw the souls of them that were beheaded for the witness of Jesus, and for the word of God, and which had not worshipped the beast, neither his image, neither had received his mark upon their foreheads, or in their hands; and they lived and reigned with Christ a thousand years. But the rest of the dead lived not again until the thousand years were finished....

11. **Revelation 20:12-15** — And I saw the dead, small and great, stand before God; and the books were opened: and another book was opened, which is the book of life: and the dead were judged out of those things which were written in the books, according to their

works. And the sea gave up the dead which were in it; and death and hell delivered up the dead which were in them: and they were judged every man according to their works. And death and hell were cast into the lake of fire. This is the second death. And whosoever was not found written in the book of life was cast into the lake of fire.

GREEK WORDS

1. "first" — (*arches*): first, beginning, or something that is elementary
2. "perfection" — (*teliotes*): moving upward into a higher dimension; pictures a student passing from one grade to the next grade
3. "foundation" — μ (*themelios*): from μ (*tithimi*), to set or position, and (*lithos*), stone; something set in stone in our lives
4. "resurrection" — (*anastasis*): a standing or rising again; a rising from the dead; resurrection

SYNOPSIS

The Church of the Holy Sepulchre, located in Jerusalem, is the site of the ancient tomb where Jesus was buried and raised from the dead more than 2,000 years ago. It stands empty because Jesus was raised from death to life by the power of the Holy Spirit!

Hebrews 6 outlines the foundations of the Christian faith, one of which is *the doctrine of the resurrection of the dead*. This is an integral "faith fundamental" we must know and understand well.

The emphasis of this lesson:

1. **The Bible clearly speaks of a future resurrection. Those who are saved, believers in Christ, have the promise of a future resurrection into eternal life. Jesus is the "first fruits" of this resurrection. This truth is the cornerstone of our Christian faith. We have a living faith because of Christ's resurrection.**
2. **Those who are not saved will also be resurrected, but it will result in eternal damnation.**

An Overview So Far

Hebrews 6:1 says, "Therefore leaving the principles of the doctrine of Christ, let us go on unto perfection." As we learned previously, the word "principles" is the Greek word *stoicheion*, which refers to *the basic elements; the fundamentals; rudimentary knowledge that is essential before advancing to higher education.*

Once you know the fundamentals of the faith and are established in them, God wants you to move beyond them unto *perfection*. The word "perfection" is the Greek word *teleiotes*, and it describes *a student who graduates from one class and moves to the next one.*

This is God's intention for you.

The writer then lists six "ABCs" of the Christian faith in verse 2: "Not laying again the foundation of repentance from dead works, and of faith toward God, of the doctrine of baptisms, and of laying on of hands, and of resurrection of the dead, and of eternal judgment."

The word "foundation" is the Greek word *themelios*, and it means *to set something in stone*. The issue of repentance — the first basic doctrine — is so vital to your faith that it should be *themelios* — set in stone — in your life.

Second in the list of foundations is "faith toward God," and we saw previously that this describes a faith that *trusts totally in God* and Christ's blood — not in church membership or good works, deeds, or anything else — to receive salvation.

"The doctrine of baptisms," the third foundational doctrine, is also crucial to your faith. There are three baptisms in the New Testament. The first is performed by the Holy Spirit the moment you are saved. The second baptism is the baptism in the Holy Spirit and is performed by Jesus. The third is water baptism, and it is conducted by believers. God desires that you personally experience all three of these baptisms.

The fourth fundamental doctrine of the Christian faith is the "laying on of hands." Understanding this element of the faith is critical to having the power God operate in your life and through your life toward others. By the laying on of hands, God's gifts of healing, authority, and *blessings of all kinds* are imparted to you and through you.

The Resurrection of the Dead

Hebrews 6:2 then lists the "resurrection of the dead." The word "resurrection" is the Greek term *anastasis*, a compound of *ana*, which means *to repeat something* or *do it again*, and the word *stasis*, which means *to stand*. When these two words are compounded, they form the word *anastasis*, signifying *to stand up again (be upright)*; *to be raised from the dead*.

This is the same word Jesus used in John 11:25 when He said, "I am the resurrection, and the life...." It was as if Jesus was saying, "I am stand-up power. If you've been knocked down or if you're dead, I have the power to put you on your feet again. I am the power that causes people to stand up again"!

Resurrection of the dead was very important when the writer of Hebrews listed it among these vital doctrines. Many believers were being killed for their faith — they literally gave their lives for Christ. Their hope of a resurrection was *vital*.

Unbelievers are naturally grieved and sorrowful when a loved one dies. Hopelessness can *engulf* them, as the grave seems to be a profound finality with no hope of eternity. But we who are believers should be filled with faith concerning the resurrection, holding to the hope that death is not the end, but only the beginning of life the way God meant it to be. We have the promise of a future resurrection unto eternal life. This is the doctrine of resurrection of the dead.

The Resurrection Is the Cornerstone of Our Faith

The apostle Paul said in First Corinthians 15:19 and 20, "If in this life only we have hope in Christ, we are of all men most miserable. But now is Christ risen from the dead, and become the firstfruits of them that slept." In other words, the fact that Christ was raised from the dead is the guarantee that we also will be raised from the dead. He was the *firstfruits* and is the promise that a harvest of resurrections will follow.

The Old Testament records three people who were resurrected from the dead. In the ministry of Jesus, three people were also resurrected from the dead. And in the book of Acts, three people were raised back to life. Yet all of these people eventually died again. They await a future resurrection. But when Christ was resurrected, He conquered death *once and for all*. He seized the keys of death and hell and will never die again!

In First Corinthians 15:3 and 4, Paul wrote, "For I delivered unto you first of all that which I also received, how that Christ died for our sins according to the scriptures; and that he was buried, and that he rose again the third day according to the scriptures."

This passage is the cornerstone of our faith. If Jesus had only died and not been resurrected, we would not have a living faith.

Christ's Post-Grave Appearances Provide Proof

Christ's resurrection was verified again and again. The Scripture says He appeared ten different times to individuals or groups of people. He first appeared to Mary Magdalene (*see* Mark 16:9-11) and then to other women (*see* Luke 24:1-10). He appeared to Peter and then to the two disciples who were walking on the road to Emmaus (*see* Luke 24:13-35). He then revealed Himself to ten of His disciples who were hiding behind locked doors (*see* John 20:19-24). Eight days later, He appeared to all 11 disciples (*see* John 20:26-30).

After that, Jesus appeared to seven of the disciples at the Sea of Tiberius (*see* John 21:1-14), and in First Corinthians 15:6, we're told He appeared to more than 500 people all at one time. In fact, many in that crowd who saw Jesus were still alive at the time Paul wrote his letter to the Corinthians. Jesus also appeared to James, His brother in the flesh, and then again to His disciples at His ascension into Heaven.

Acts 1:3 records that Jesus showed "himself alive after his passion by many infallible proofs, being seen of *them* forty days, and speaking of the things pertaining to the kingdom of God." The word "them" refers to a vast number of people who saw Him. His several, repeated appearances were undeniable proof that He was raised from the dead.

Three Resurrections To Come

Jesus spoke of two different resurrections for two separate groups of people that are going to take place in the future. In John 5:29, He said, "And shall come forth; they that have done good, unto the resurrection of life; and they that have done evil, unto the resurrection of damnation."

There is going to be a resurrection of the righteous — those who have been saved because they made Christ their Lord and Savior. There will also be a resurrection of the unrighteous — those who are not saved. This truth is taught throughout Scripture.

There will actually be two resurrections for the righteous. The **first resurrection of the righteous** will occur simultaneously at the rapture or the "catching away" of the Church. Believers who have already died will at that moment be raised from the dead. Then believers who are alive at that time will be caught up to meet the Lord in the air. The apostle Paul wrote about this in First Thessalonians 4:15-18:

> "For this we say unto you by the word of the Lord, that we which are alive and remain unto the coming of the Lord shall not prevent them which are asleep. For the Lord himself shall descend from heaven with a shout, with the voice of the archangel, and with the trump of God: and the dead in Christ shall rise first: then we which are alive and remain shall be caught up together with them in the clouds, to meet the Lord in the air: and so shall we ever be with the Lord. Wherefore comfort one another with these words."

Paul confirmed this first resurrection in First Corinthians 15:51-53:

> "Behold, I shew you a mystery; we shall not all sleep, but we shall all be changed, in a moment, in the twinkling of an eye, at the last trump: for the trumpet shall sound, and the dead shall be raised incorruptible, and we shall be changed. For this corruptible must put on incorruption, and this mortal must put on immortality."

Then in Philippians 3:20 and 21 (*NKJV*), Paul affirmed the resurrection of the righteous a third time:

> "For our citizenship is in heaven, from which we also eagerly wait for the Savior, the Lord Jesus Christ, who will transform our lowly body that it may be conformed to His glorious body, according to the working by which He is able even to subdue all things to Himself."

As believers, we eagerly await the coming of the Lord when He will gather us all at the time of the rapture. In that moment, He will transform our physical bodies into resurrected bodies just like His.

There will also be a **second resurrection for the righteous** who died for their faith during the Great Tribulation, and it will happen at the end of that tribulation period. Scripture talks about this in Revelation 20:4:

> "And I saw thrones, and they sat upon them, and judgment was given unto them: and I saw the souls of them that were beheaded for the witness of Jesus, and for the word of God, and which had not worshipped the beast, neither his image, neither had received his mark upon their foreheads, or in their hands; and they lived and reigned with Christ a thousand years."

Those who are saved and give their lives for Christ during the Tribulation will live again. They will be resurrected and will reign with Jesus for a thousand years.

The **third resurrection** the Bible mentions is for the *unsaved* (unrighteous), and it is spoken of in Revelation 20:5. It says, "But the rest of the dead lived not again until the thousand years were finished...." The apostle John expounds on this in verses 12-15:

> "And I saw the dead, small and great, stand before God; and the books were opened: and another book was opened, which is the book of life: and the dead were judged out of those things which were written in the books, according to their works. And the sea gave up the dead which were in it; and death and hell delivered up the dead which were in them: and they were judged every man according to their works. And death and hell were cast into the lake of fire. This is the second death. And whosoever was not found written in the book of life was cast into the lake of fire."

The resurrection of the unrighteous will occur before the Great White Throne Judgment at the very end of the millennial reign of Christ. All those who are unsaved from the beginning of creation to the end of the Tribulation will be summoned to stand before God and be judged.

If you are in Christ, you will not stand in this judgment. Jesus is the *first fruits* of the resurrection of the righteous. He is the guarantee of the harvest of people who will be resurrected in the days ahead.

STUDY QUESTIONS

**Study to shew thyself approved unto God, a workman that needeth
not to be ashamed, rightly dividing the word of truth.
— 2 Timothy 2:15**

Resurrection from the dead to eternal life in Heaven is the *blessed hope* of every believer. Eternal life is promised by Christ Himself (*see* John 3:16) and is woven like a tapestry throughout the New Testament. Take time to look over these passages: Titus 3:3-8; 1 Peter 1:3-7; Acts 24:15; and Hebrews 6:18, 19.

1. What would your life be like without the promised hope of eternal life in Heaven? (*Consider* First Corinthians 15:12-19; 29-32.)
2. How does the promise of being resurrected, receiving a glorified body, and living forever in Heaven with Jesus encourage you to live for Him each day? (*Consider* First Corinthians 15:42-44, 50-55 and Philippians 3:20, 21.)

PRACTICAL APPLICATION

**But be ye doers of the word, and not hearers only,
deceiving your own selves.
— James 1:22**

1. The Bible talks about both a resurrection for the *righteous* in Christ as well as a resurrection of the *unrighteous* — those who are not saved. How has this lesson given you new understanding about the resurrection that awaits *you* as a believer?
2. After hearing the scriptures on what awaits the unrighteous, how are you motivated to share the Gospel with those who are lost around you? (For review, *consider* John 5:29 and Revelation 20:11-15.)

LESSON 7

TOPIC
The Doctrine of Eternal Judgment

SCRIPTURES
1. **Hebrews 5:12** — For when for the time ye ought to be teachers, ye have need that one teach you again which be the first principles of the oracles of God; and are become such as have need of milk, and me of strong meat.
2. **Hebrews 6:1, 2** — Therefore leaving the principles of the doctrine of Christ, let us go on unto perfection; not laying again the foundation of repentance from dead works, and of faith toward God, of the doctrine of baptisms, and of laying on of hands, and of resurrection of the dead, and of eternal judgment.
3. **Revelation 20:11-15** — And I saw a great white throne, and him that sat on it, from whose face the earth and the heaven fled away; and there was found no place for them. And I saw the dead, small and great, stand before God; and the books were opened: and another book was opened, which is the book of life: and the dead were judged out of those things which were written in the books, according to their works. And the sea gave up the dead which were in it; and death and hell delivered up the dead which were in them: and they were judged every man according to their works. And death and hell were cast into the lake of fire. This is the second death. And whosoever was not found written in the book of life was cast into the lake of fire.
4. **Romans 8:1** — There is therefore now no condemnation to them which are in Christ Jesus, who walk not after the flesh, but after the Spirit.
5. **Romans 14:10, 12** — ...For we shall all stand before the judgment seat of Christ. So then every one of us shall give an account of himself to God.
6. **2 Corinthians 5:10** — For we must all appear before the judgement seat of Christ; that every one may receive the things done in his body, according to that he hath done, whether it be good of bad.

7. **1 Corinthians 3:13** — Every man's work shall be made manifest: for the day shall declare it, because it shall be revealed by fire; and the fire shall try every man's work of what sort it is
8. **Matthew 25:19** — After a long time the lord of those servants cometh, and reckoneth with them.

GREEK WORDS

1. "first" — (*arches*): first, beginning, or something that is elementary
2. "perfection" — (*teliotes*): moving upward into a higher dimension; pictures a student passing from one grade to the next grade
3. "stand" — ϖ μ (*paristemi*): to stand, not crawl or grovel; "there will be no shame here"
4. "judgment seat" — μ (*bema*): a platform on which a judge or governor gave judgment or rewards; a place of evaluation and designation
5. "appear" — (*phaneros*): apparent; revealed or visible; manifest
6. "each one" — (*hekastos*): it is all inclusive, no one excluded
7. "receive" — μ (*komidzo*): to receive what is due or what one has coming to him
8. "reckoned" — μ (*logidzomai*): a bookkeeping term that means to compare accounts; pictures an accountant who put together a profit and loss statement; a thorough examination of books

SYNOPSIS

In upper Ephesus lies the remains of what once was a thriving marketplace. It was a destination the affluent visited regularly. Close by was the Basilica, which was a huge building filled with statues and paintings. At any time of the day or week, one could find the wealthy enjoying this beautiful area of the city. But today, all that remains are the foundational stones upon which this magnificent marketplace once stood.

As we continue this series on the foundations of faith, we have opportunity to stop and think, *What kind of a foundation do I have personally?* It was written about the Hebrew believers, "…Ye ought to be teachers, [but] ye have need that one teach you again which be the first principles of the oracles of God…" (Hebrews 5:12). Those believers had heard much preaching and had seen the powerful workings of the Holy Spirit. They should have been "teachers," from the Greek word *didaskalos*, which means they should have been on the spiritual level of a rabbi with an obligation to teach others what they'd studied. Instead, they needed to be taught again the "first principles of the oracles of God."

As already noted, this word "first" is from the Greek word *arche*, and it refers to *the beginning or starting point of something*. In this context, the writer was speaking by the inspiration of the Holy Spirit about the ABCs — the fundamentals — of the faith.

You need to know your ABCs! These foundational truths in Hebrews 6:1 and 2 are essential for establishing a solid, stable foundation to build your life on. Without this kind of foundation, you will end up making tragic mistakes at some time or another in your life.

The emphasis of this lesson:

There are two future judgments coming. Those who are unsaved will appear before God's White Throne Judgment. And believers will stand before the judgment seat of Christ. Those who are saved and in Christ will *not* appear before the Great White Throne Judgment. Nevertheless, our works as believers will be thoroughly examined and tried. Christ will then designate how we are to be rewarded. Hence, the way we build and steward our lives on earth will have an effect for all eternity.

Hebrews 6:1 and 2 says, "Therefore leaving the principles of the doctrine of Christ, let us go on unto perfection; not laying again the foundation of repentance from dead works, and of faith toward God, of the doctrine of baptisms, and of laying on of hands, and of resurrection of the dead, and of eternal judgment."

So far, we've covered five of the six foundational teachings listed in these verses. They are as follows:

1. **Repentance from dead works.** "Repentance" means *a change of mind*; *a complete conversion*; *a turn or a new course*; or *a completely altered view of life and behavior*.
2. **Faith toward God.** This word "faith" describes a faith that is rooted and rests in Christ alone.

3. **The doctrine of baptisms.** The word "baptisms" is plural because there are three baptisms in the New Testament, and God wants you to experience all of them.
4. **The laying on of hands.** Well established throughout Scripture, this doctrine expresses God's desire and plan to use human hands to impart blessing — not only the blessing of His power, but His many gifts as well.
5. **The resurrection of the dead.** There are three resurrections in the future. The first is for those who are saved. It will occur simultaneously with the rapture or the "catching away" of the Church. All believers who die before that time will be raised from the dead in that moment. The second resurrection will occur at the end of the Great Tribulation, and it will be for those who accepted Christ and gave their lives for Him during the Tribulation. The third and final resurrection will be for the unsaved. This resurrection will take place at the very end of the millennial reign of Christ.

Eternal Judgment for the Unrighteous: The Great White Throne

The *sixth* foundational teaching listed in Hebrews 6:2 is "eternal judgment," which consists of two different judgments. The first is for the unsaved and is often referred to as the White Throne Judgment. The Bible talks about this in Revelation 20:11-15.

> "And I saw a great white throne, and him that sat on it, from whose face the earth and the heaven fled away; and there was found no place for them. And I saw the dead, small and great, stand before God; and the books were opened: and another book was opened, which is the book of life: and the dead were judged out of those things which were written in the books, according to their works. And the sea gave up the dead which were in it; and death and hell delivered up the dead which were in them: and they were judged every man according to their works. And death and hell were cast into the lake of fire. This is the second death. And whosoever was not found written in the book of life was cast into the lake of fire."

Scripture says God has "books" about every person's life. At this judgment for the unrighteous, these books will be opened and people will be judged "according to their works." Whoever's name is not found written in the "book of life" will be cast into the lake of fire. This judgment, which will take place at the end of the millennial reign of Christ, is not for believers but for unbelievers.

Eternal Judgment for the Righteous: The Judgment Seat of Christ

Believers will also experience a judgment, but it will be more a time of evaluation and designation. Remember, for those who are saved, "there is therefore now no condemnation to them which are in Christ Jesus, who walk not after the flesh, but after the Spirit" (Romans 8:1). When we stand before God, He is not going to deal with us about sin. We have already confessed and repented of our sins, and they are "under the blood" of Jesus, supernaturally washed away by His cleansing power. We are forever forgiven of those sins, and God will remember them no more (*see* Psalm 103:12).

In Romans 14:10, the apostle Paul talked about the final judgment for believers. He said, "…For we shall all stand before the judgment seat of Christ." The word "stand" is the Greek word *paristemi*, which means *to stand, not crawl or grovel*. This signifies that there will be no shame there whatsoever.

Interestingly, the word judgment is not in the original text. The phrase rendered "judgment seat" in Romans 14:10 is the Greek word *bema,* and it describes *a platform on which a judge or governor gave judgment*. The word *bema* was taken from the ancient Greek Isthmian games in which athletes competed for a reward. As they competed, they were under the careful scrutiny of judges who watched to make sure every rule of the contest was obeyed. After the games had ended, the victors were led to a platform, which was called the *bema*. The bema was the place where the judge placed laurel crowns on the heads of those who had fought well.

By using the word *bema*, Paul depicts believers as competitors in a spiritual contest. And just as victorious athletes appeared before the *bema* to receive a physical reward, Christians will one day appear before Christ's *bema* to receive an incorruptible, spiritual reward. His *bema* will not be a place where losers are punished. It will be a place where all believers' works will be evaluated, and those who fought and competed well — according to the "rules" of His Word and His will — will be rewarded.

Romans 14:12 says, "So then every one of us shall give an account of himself to God." The phrase "give account" means we are each going to give a factual report of what we did and did not do. We will stand before Christ, and it will be revealed whether we "played by the rules" and did what He told us to do.

In Second Corinthians 5:10, Paul wrote virtually the same thing: "For we must all appear before the judgement seat of Christ; that every one may receive the things done in his body, according to that he hath done, whether it be good of bad." The word "appear" is the Greek word *phaneros*, which means *apparent, revealed, visible,* or *manifest.* When you stand before the judgment seat (the *bema*) of Christ, what you have done in your walk of faith will be clearly *revealed.*

Also in this verse is the phrase "every one" — the Greek word *hekastos,* meaning *all-inclusive; no one excluded.* Every single believer will appear before the *bema* of Christ. It doesn't matter who you are or how long you've been saved — you will stand before Jesus to have your works evaluated.

The Bible then says we will "receive the things done in [the] body." The word "receive" is the Greek word *komidzo,* and it means *to receive what is due or what one has coming to him.* If you have worked hard for the Lord, you will have a reward coming to you. If you haven't worked hard, you may not have much coming your way.

Tried By Fire

First Corinthians 3:10-13 also sheds light on the *bema* seat of Christ. Verse 13 says, "Every man's work shall be made manifest: for the day shall declare it, because it shall be revealed by fire; and the fire shall try every man's work of what sort it is." The phrase, "revealed by fire" carries the idea of our works being tested through an intense examination. *What* we built for the Kingdom of God and *why* we built it will be put to the test.

If we weren't obedient or we didn't do what the Lord told us to do, our works will go up in flames. If we were obedient and our motivation for what we did was right, we will receive a reward. Regardless of what happens to our works, we will be saved. Our salvation is not based on our works, but on the finished work of Jesus Christ and His shed blood.

Jesus Himself talked about the time believers' works would be evaluated. This discourse can be found in the parable of the talents in Matthew 25.

The master gave each of his servants talents to invest. He went away for a time and then returned to examine the fruit of their efforts. Verse 19 says, "After a long time the lord of those servants cometh, and reckoneth with them." The word "reckoneth" is the Greek word *logidzomai*. It is a bookkeeping term that means *to compare accounts*, and it pictures *an accountant who put together a profit-and-loss statement and performed a thorough examination of the books*.

When you stand before the *bema* seat of Christ, He is going to compare what He gave you with what you ultimately produced. Did you increase it or did it stay the same? Once He has evaluated what you did with the gifts and talents He gave you, He will designate what kind of reward you should receive.

Five Crowns

Five specific crowns are mentioned in Scripture that will be given to faithful believers:

1. The **Crown of Incorruption.** This reward is referred to in First Corinthians 9:25. This "crown of incorruption" will be given to believers who practice self-discipline.
2. The **Crown of Rejoicing.** This reward is mentioned in First Thessalonians 2:19 and is often called the "soul-winner's crown."
3. The **Crown of Righteousness.** Second Timothy 4:8 talks about this reward for believers who are longing for Jesus' appearance and living a holy life in anticipation of His return.
4. The **Crown of Glory.** Referred to in First Peter 5:4, this reward is often called the "pastor's crown" because it will be given to pastors for being faithful in the care of the congregation they have overseen.
5. The **Crown of Life.** James 1:12 and Revelation 2:10 speaks of the "martyr's crown" because it is a reward for those who suffered for their faith and remained faithful.

STUDY QUESTIONS

> Study to shew thyself approved unto God, a workman that needeth not to be ashamed, rightly dividing the word of truth.
> — 2 Timothy 2:15

1. Romans 4:10 and 12 says, "...For we shall all stand before the judgment seat of Christ.... So then every one of us shall give an account of himself to God." This truth is confirmed in other places in Scripture (*see* 2 Corinthians 5:10; Hebrews 4:13). What does the realization of this coming day of reckoning speak to you personally?
2. The Bible talks about the Book of Life in which God has written the names of all who believe on Jesus Christ. There is another book that He will open at the end of time, and it is mentioned in Malachi 3:16-18. Give the name of this book and tell what God is recording in it. What does this passage specifically encourage you to do?

PRACTICAL APPLICATION

But be ye doers of the word, and not hearers only, deceiving your own selves.
—James 1:22

1. As a believer, you will one day stand before the judgment seat (*bema*) of Christ, and all your life's works will be thoroughly examined and tested. How does being aware of this evaluation shape and direct your service for Jesus? What adjustments does it motivate you to make in your life?
2. Not only will your earthly accomplishments for Christ be examined, your *motives* for carrying out each assignment will also be put to the test (*see* Luke 12:2; 1 Corinthians 4:5). In light of this knowledge, write out a brief prayer, inviting the Holy Spirit to purify your motives and instill in you the reverential fear of the Lord.
3. The testing of works "by fire" implies that it's not just working for the Lord that counts, but rather doing the works that *He* has assigned you to do. Does this knowledge inspire you to press in to find and fulfill His perfect will for your life? Is there something you know He has asked of you that you have been hesitant to carry out? Are you too busy working for the Lord that you can't seem to find time to do the things you *know* He has put on your heart to do? Answer these questions honestly and seek Him for a plan to rectify any wrong direction or turns your life has taken, even though it may have been with the best of intentions.

LESSON 8

TOPIC
A Transplant That Will Save Your Life

SCRIPTURES
1. **Hebrews 6:1, 2** — Therefore leaving the principles of the doctrine of Christ, let us go on unto perfection; not laying again the foundation of repentance from dead works, and of faith toward God, of the doctrine of baptisms, and of laying on of hands, and of resurrection of the dead, and of eternal judgment.
2. **James 1:21** — Wherefore lay apart all filthiness and superfluity of naughtiness, and receive with meekness the engrafted word, which is able to save your souls.

GREEK WORDS
1. "lay apart" — ϖ μ (*apotithimi*): to lay something down; to lay something down and push it beyond reach so that it cannot be easily retrieved; to lay something down and to push beyond reach; a deliberate decision to make a permanent change of attitude and behavior; can be used to denote the removal of clothes
2. "filthiness" — ϖ (*rhuparia*): filthy; vile; soiled; dirty; obnoxiously filthy; especially used to denote filthy and smelly clothes; something that is base
3. "superfluity" — ϖ (*perissos*): excessive; exceedingly; something so profuse that it can be likened to a river that is overflowing and flooding its banks
4. "naughtiness" — (*kakia*): bad; evil; vile; foul
5. "engrafted" — μ (*emphutos*): engrafted; subsequently implanted
6. "meekness" — ϖ (*prautes*): a strong-willed person who has learned to submit his will to a higher authority
7. "save" — (*sodzo*): salvation; wholeness in every part of life in an eternal or temporal sense; salvation that brings delivering and healing power that results in wholeness; can be translated *to heal*

SYNOPSIS

The ancient city of Ephesus was home to the third-largest library in the world during the Second Century. The Celsus Library was a place of education and learning that drew people from all over the continent of Asia.

Interestingly, the apostle Paul taught the Word of God just a few steps away from the Celsus Library in what was called the School of Tyrannus (*see* Acts 19:8-12). Paul knew people needed to be firmly established on the foundation of God's Word, and the same is true for us today.

The ABCs of the Christian Faith

Hebrews 6:1 says, "Therefore leaving the principles of the doctrine of Christ, let us go on unto perfection…." Again, this word "perfection" is from the Greek word *teleiotes*, and it describes a student who graduates from one level of education to the next.

This is God's intention and invitation for you — to learn the elementary principles of Christianity and then to move beyond them to spiritual maturity. He desires your continual advancement in spiritual things, growth in your maturity in Christ, and forward movement so that you are not perpetually "stuck" in your walk with Him.

What are the "principles of the doctrine of Christ"? Hebrews 6:1, 2 lists them as follows:

1. Repentance from dead works
2. Faith toward God
3. Doctrine of baptisms
4. Laying on of hands
5. Resurrection of the dead
6. Eternal judgment

From what you've previously read and heard, use the space that follows to write out for yourself a brief description of these basic doctrines.

Repentance From Dead Works _____
_____
_____
_____
_____

Faith Toward God _____
_____
_____
_____
_____

Doctrine of Baptisms _____
_____
_____
_____
_____

Laying on of Hands _____
_____
_____
_____
_____

Resurrection of the Dead _____
_____
_____
_____
_____

Eternal Judgment _____
_____
_____
_____
_____

These six doctrines are the elementary principles of Christ — the ABCs of the Christian faith.

The emphasis of this lesson:

Stubborn areas of our thinking, believing, and behavior that are contrary to God's Word "stink" spiritually! God instructs us to push them out of our reach before their influence infiltrates and negatively affects every area of our lives. As we receive God's Word with meekness, its

inherent power will bring healing and wholeness to our entire beings and lives.

What It Means to 'Lay Apart' Something in Your Life

An important aspect of building our lives on a solid foundation is found in James 1:21.

> "Wherefore lay apart all filthiness and superfluity of naughtiness, and receive with meekness the engrafted word, which is able to save your souls."

This verse tells us what we need to do in order to truly receive and absorb the Word of God into our lives and not just be superficial hearers of the Word.

James writes, "…Lay apart all filthiness and superfluity of naughtiness…." The phrase "lay apart" is from the Greek word *apotithimi*, and it means *to lay something down and push it beyond reach so that it cannot be easily retrieved*. It is a deliberate decision to make a permanent change of *attitude* and *behavior*. In fact, *apotithimi* is the same Greek word used to depict the removal of old, dirty clothes.

When you come to the end of your day and it's time to get ready for bed, what do you do to remove the clothes you've been wearing all day? You don't stand in front of the mirror and say, "Okay, clothes, I'm done with you. Come off my body this instant!" Of course, it doesn't work that way. To remove the clothes you're wearing to put on other garments, you must first use your hands and fingers to remove those "old" clothes from your body. You choose to unzip the zippers or push the buttons through the button holes, and you purposely remove what you've been wearing.

Essentially, James told us that when we hear the Word of God and we come to the realization that an area in our life doesn't line up with the Word, we have to decide to "take off" or remove what is wrong. Simply recognizing that something in us is not right will not bring change. We have to *make a decision* and *take action*. This is actually repentance — deciding to embrace the truth and to change something in our lives or to turn from a wrong direction in which we were headed.

Apotithimi (lay apart) is the compound of two words — *apo* and *tithimi* — that means *to put enough space between you and that old, dirty thing in your life that you cannot easily reach over and pick it up again*. When you have done something for a long time, it becomes a habit, and it is very easy to pick that habit back up and continue in it. In order to make a permanent break from patterns of wrong thinking and behavior, you have to "lay it apart" — push it far enough away from you that you can't reach it and put it back on again.

'Filthiness and Superfluity of Naughtiness' — What Is That?

What are we to "lay apart"? James said, "…filthiness and superfluity of naughtiness…" (James 1:21). The word "filthiness" is the Greek word *rhuparia*, and it describes *something obnoxiously filthy, vile, or soiled; something that is extremely base*. *Rhuparia* is especially used to denote filthy, smelly clothes.

When we have a way of thinking, believing, or acting that is wrong — and we allow it to continue in our lives unchecked — God's Word says it stinks with an unbearable stench. If we know that what we are thinking, believing, or doing goes against God's Word, it is a type of grimy filthiness that we need to "lay apart" from our lives.

We are also told to lay apart "superfluity of naughtiness." The word "superfluity" is from the Greek word *perissos*, which describes *something excessive and so profuse that it can be likened to a swollen river that is overflowing and flooding its banks*. In other words, if we don't get a grip on what is wrong in our lives, it will become worse and worse until it eventually flows into every area of our lives.

"Naughtiness" is from the Greek word *kakia*, meaning *something bad, evil, foul,* or *rank*. It is putrid and has a dreadful stench. Once a believer comes to the realization that his thoughts, words, or actions are wrong, he has a choice to make. He can remain in that situation because it requires too much effort to change, or he can do whatever is necessary to break free.

Instead of tolerating "filthiness and superfluity of naughtiness" in our lives, we are to obey God's instruction to take them off, lay them down, and push them so far away that we cannot reach them to pick them up again.

Receive the 'Engrafted' Word With Meekness

As we "lay apart filthiness and superfluity of naughtiness," James also instructed us by the inspiration of the Spirit to "receive with meekness the engrafted word, which is able to save your souls" (James 1:21). The term "engrafted" is the Greek word *emphutos*, and it describes *something that is engrafted, or implanted, in us later in life*. It is not something with which we were born.

The best illustration of this word "engrafted" (*emphutos*) is someone undergoing an organ transplant. If a major organ in your body — such as your heart — were to fail, you would not live unless you received another one. The heart you receive would not be from your body originally. It would be a transplanted heart from another body. And your body would need to accept that heart and not reject it. In a sense, your body would have to receive that organ with "meekness."

"Meekness" is the Greek word *prautes*. It is the picture of *a strong-willed person who has learned to submit his will to a higher authority*. He has decided to deny his own thoughts, feelings, and beliefs and to deliberately submit to someone else in order to receive what he has to say or to impart.

Essentially, James was saying that the only way God's Word will take root in you and save your soul is if you receive it with "meekness" (*prautes*). That is, you have to say no to your own opinions, views, and ways, and open your heart to hear and obey the Word.

Five Steps To Have the Word Effectively Transplanted in You

Submission: You have to be *submitted* to the authority of God. You have to purposely choose to come under His authority, believe what He says in His Word, and then do it, regardless of what you think or how you feel.

Elimination: You must then *eliminate* your own opinion and feelings and anything else that would distract or keep you from submitting to God's authority. Take them off — lay them apart — and do not reach to pick back up thoughts that would keep you from submitting to and aligning yourself with God.

Decision: *Decide* that you will not veer from what God says, but that you will instead remain committed to the principles of His Word.

Continuation: Your decision is not a one-time event, but an ongoing commitment to *continually* deny yourself, eliminate wrong thinking, and remain in submission to the Word of God.

Reception: As you walk out the first four steps, you will finally begin to *receive* the Word of God into your life, which "is able to save your souls." The word "able" is from the Greek word *dunamis*, which means *power*. The power of God's Word will actively be at work in you, saving your soul — your mind, your will, and your emotions.

The word "save" is the Greek word *sodzo*, meaning *salvation*. The saving power of the Word brings *deliverance and healing that results in wholeness in every part of your life in an eternal or temporal sense.*

When you live in submission to God's Word, eliminate wrong thinking and believing, and decide to obey the Word and continue in it, a flood of divine power will be released in you. The Word will begin to take root and work to preserve your life.

QUESTIONS

> **Study to shew thyself approved unto God, a workman that needeth not to be ashamed, rightly dividing the word of truth.**
> **— 2 Timothy 2:15**

1. James 1:21 says we're to "receive with meekness the engrafted word, which is able to save your souls." How powerful is the Word of God in your life? Read Romans 1:16, Hebrews 4:12, and Jeremiah 23:28, 29. Then describe what the Word is working in you.
2. The five steps for God's Word to effectively be "transplanted" in you are *submission, elimination, decision, continuation,* and *reception*. Of the first four, which one(s) do you need the Holy Spirit's help with most? Take a moment to pray and invite Him into the situation you're facing.

PRACTICAL APPLICATION

> **But be ye doers of the word, and not hearers only, deceiving your own selves.**
> **— James 1:22**

1. "Filthiness" describes *something filthy, vile, soiled,* or *extremely base*. Pause and pray, "Lord, is there an area in my thinking, believing, or behavior that You would call *filthiness*? If so, what is it?" Write what He reveals.
2. We are also told to lay apart "superfluity of naughtiness." This is something so *excessively bad or evil* that if we don't deal with it, it will *overflow* and begin to affect the other areas of our life. Again, take a moment to pray: "Lord, is there an area in my life that falls into this category? If so, what is it?" Write anything He shows you.
3. To "lay apart" means *to lay something down and push it beyond your reach so that it cannot be easily retrieved*. It is *a* deliberate decision to make a permanent change in your *attitude* and *behavior*. In light of your answers to the previous questions, pause and ask the Lord what practical steps you can take to *lay apart* the things that are contaminating your life. Write what He reveals to you.

LESSON 9

TOPIC
Are You Just a Listener or Are You a Disciple?

SCRIPTURES

1. **Hebrews 6:1, 2** — Therefore leaving the principles of the doctrine of Christ, let us go on unto perfection; not laying again the foundation of repentance from dead works, and of faith toward God, of the doctrine of baptisms, and of laying on of hands, and of resurrection of the dead, and of eternal judgment.
2. **James 1:21, 22** — Wherefore lay apart all filthiness and superfluity of naughtiness, and receive with meekness the engrafted word, which is able to save your souls. But be ye doers of the word, and not hearers only, deceiving your own selves.

GREEK WORDS

1. "meekness" — ϖ (*prautes*): a strong-willed person who has learned to submit his will to a higher authority
2. "engrafted" — μ (*emphutos*): engrafted; subsequently implanted
3. "save" — (*sodzo*): salvation; wholeness in every part of life in an eternal or temporal sense; salvation that brings delivering and healing power that results in wholeness; can be translated to heal
4. "souls" — (*psuche*): a person's mind, will, and emotions, which New Testament writers clearly understood to be components of the soul; the inner life, mental makeup, or emotions of an individual; the mental or emotional realm
5. "doers" — ϖ (*poieo*): to do; to do creatively; to perform; the root for the word poet
6. "hearers only" — (*akroates*): used to describe individuals who audited a class rather than take it for credit; hence, it depicted a hearer only, or one who had no intention of applying what he heard; he merely attended the class but had no plans to implement what was taught
7. "deceiving" — ϖ μ (*paralogidzomai*): a miscalculation; a wrong analysis of facts or of a situation

SYNOPSIS

In the heart of the ancient city of Ephesus was Philosopher's Square, the Celsus Library, and the School of Tyrannus where the apostle Paul taught the Word of God for more than two years. Acts 19 indicates that every day of the week, in the morning and afternoon, he explained the Scriptures to people who came from all over Asia. Many of them had been saved out of a life of paganism and had no concept of right and wrong. Paul believed they needed a foundation on which to build their lives. And regardless of our own backgrounds, the same is true for us today.

We need to know and understand what the Bible teaches about our Christian faith. As followers of Christ, we are called to be His "disciples," which in Greek is the word *mathetes*, meaning *committed learners*. God wants us to be committed to *hear*, *learn*, and *do* what the Word teaches.

The emphasis of this lesson:

As disciples of Christ, we are called to be *committed learners* who are not just hearers of the Word, but who are also *committed doers* of the Word. We are to receive God's truth with meekness and put it into practice by whatever creative means necessary to make it a part of our life that bears fruit.

'Receive With Meekness the Engrafted Word'

In the past several lessons, we thoroughly examined six foundational doctrines outlined in Hebrews 6:1 and 2. We also touched on James 1:21 in our last lesson, which says, "Wherefore lay apart all filthiness and superfluity of naughtiness, and receive with meekness the engrafted word, which is able to save your souls."

The phrase "receive with meekness" is very important. Often when people hear the word *meek*, they think it means *weak*, but that is not what this word means. The word "meekness" here is from the Greek word *prautes*, and it describes *a strong-willed person who thinks he is right, but has learned to submit his will to a higher authority*. That is, he has chosen to deny what he thinks and how he feels about things and to deliberately put his trust in someone else in order to prosper and receive from that person.

What are we to receive with meekness? James said, "The engrafted word, which is able to save your souls." The word "engrafted" is *emphutos*, and it signifies *something that is planted in you at a later time in life; it is something with which you were not born*.

The best illustration of the word "engrafted" is someone who undergoes an organ transplant. If you're in need of a new organ, you're in a pretty serious situation. In fact, you could die if you don't get a new one. When you receive a donated organ, it is not yours — that is, it's an organ from another source that is placed in you. Interestingly, upon receiving the new organ, the body will immediately attempt to reject it. Innately, the body knows the organ is not original to that body, and it begins treating it as a foreign object. Deliberate measures must be taken for the body to receive the new organ. All of this imagery is packed into the word "engrafted" (*emphutos*).

God's Word Has Saving Power

Scripture says the "engrafted" Word of God "is able to save your souls." The word "save" is the Greek word *sodzo*, which means *salvation; wholeness in every part of life in an eternal or temporal sense*. The Word brings salvation that releases *delivering and healing power* resulting in *wholeness*. That is what the power of God's Word will do in your soul.

"Souls" is the Greek word *psuche*, and it describes *a person's mind, will, and emotions*. New Testament writers clearly understood these to be components of the soul or inner life. And where do we need the greatest transformation in our lives? In the realm of the soul — the mind, will, and emotions.

Think about what happens when you hear the Word of God. The truths come into you like a donated organ that is desperately needed to save your life. Yet as these godly principles and truths enter your soul, an internal alarm is sometimes sounded. It is as if your mind says, *Wait a minute! These principles go against my established belief system and what I've learned in the past.*

Then your emotions chime in, *This just doesn't feel right. What I'm hearing makes me uncomfortable*. Similar to the way the human body reacts to receiving an organ transplant, your soul will at times attempt to reject the Word of God.

In order for a transplanted organ to be accepted and take root in a person's body, that person has to take medication — often for the rest of his or her life. Because the "engrafted" organ is foreign to the body, the body often attempts to reject it. However, if the patient stays on the medication and submits to the wise care of his doctor, the organ will be likely accepted and begin to function properly, saving the person's life.

This is precisely what we must do with the Word of God. We must willfully and deliberately submit to the wise and tender care of God's Word.

A Review of the Five Steps for Receiving the Engrafted Word

Submission: You must continuously live in *submission* to the Word of God in order for its power to be released in your life.

Elimination: You must *eliminate* anything that tries to keep you from submitting to the Word, including outside voices and opinions, as well as your own opposing thoughts, feelings, and desires.

Decision: Make a *decision* that you are going to live in submission to the Word for the long haul.

Continuation: Living in submission is not something you just do once. It is a decision to *continually* receive the word with meekness, regardless of whether it feels natural or comfortable.

Reception: As you decide to continually live in submission to God's Word, eliminating anything tries to keep you from obeying it, the saving power of the Word will take effect. You will begin experiencing positive change in every area of your life.

Be a *Doer*, Not Just a *Hearer*

James 1:22 says, "But be ye doers of the word, and not hearers only, deceiving your own selves." In the Greek, "be ye doers" essentially means *be ye becoming*. In other words, *start where you are* and begin doing something in obedience to what the Word says.

The word "doer" is the Greek word *poieo*, and it means *to creatively do something*. It is where we get the word "poet." A poet has a creative flare for expressing thoughts and ideas. By using the word *poieo*, the Bible is saying, "Don't wait until it is convenient or easy to obey the Word. Find a way to creatively do what God says to do." Remember, you are a "disciple" — a *committed learner* of Christ who is listening to, learning, and applying His teachings.

We are to be "doers of the word, and not hearers only." The phrase "hearers only" is from the Greek word *akroates*. This term was used to describe *individuals who audited a class rather than taking it for credit*. Hence, it depicted *a hearer only* or *one who had no intention of applying what he heard*. This person merely attended the class, but had no serious plans to implement what was taught.

James 1:21 tells us that there are two kinds of Christians: The first is a *doer*, or one who hears the Word of God and does whatever he can to creatively obey what it says. The second is a *hearer only* — one who shows up and is physically present to hear the Word, but mentally and spiritually, he is disengaged. That is, he has no serious intentions of doing what the Word says.

James 1:22 concludes with the words "deceiving your own selves." The word "deceiving" is the Greek word *paralogidzomai*, which essentially means *to make a miscalculation*. It is a library term that depicts a scholar placing documents side-by-side to compare and analyze the information. If he made the wrong analysis of the facts or situation, it was called a *paralogidzomai*.

Basically, James is saying, "If you think things are going to improve and be great just because you *hear* the Word, you have made a tragic miscalculation — your analysis is wrong." Yes, you need to hear the Word, but you must also find a way to creatively put it into practice. You are called by Christ to be His "disciple" (*mathetes*) — a committed learner who *does* what he *hears*.

STUDY QUESTIONS

> Study to shew thyself approved unto God, a workman that needeth not to be ashamed, rightly dividing the word of truth.
> — 2 Timothy 2:15

1. Many times, an instruction in one area of Scripture is repeated in another. Such is the case with James 1:21 and Hebrews 12:1, 2. Carefully read these two passages. In what ways are they *alike*? Can you think of any other passages with a similar directive?
2. According to James 1:21, the Word of God contains the *power* to save your soul. Your mind, will, and emotions can be transformed by the truth of Scripture. Look back over your life and name one or two areas in your thinking or behavior that have been changed by God's Word. Describe how things changed and tell what verses played a part in the process.

PRACTICAL APPLICATION

> But be ye doers of the word, and not hearers only, deceiving your own selves.
> — James 1:22

1. Just as a person's physical body will often attempt to reject a transplanted organ, your soul will often attempt to reject the Word of God from being "engrafted" into your inner life. Think about it. What are some of the internal objections (thoughts, reasonings, and feelings) your soul voices in an effort to keep the truth from taking root in you? How does this lesson motivate you to stand against these arguments and others like them?
2. The word "doer" is from the Greek word *poieo*, and it pictures *creativity*. If you could name the greatest area in which you are struggling to obey God, what would it be? What are some practical, creative steps you can take to help you obey God's Word and avoid falling into this recurring area of disobedience?

LESSON 10

TOPIC

Understanding Your Spiritual Level

SCRIPTURES
1. **James 1:22-25** —But be ye doers of the word, and not hearers only, deceiving your own selves. For if any be a hearer of the word, and not a doer, he is like unto a man beholding his natural face in a glass: for he beholdeth himself, and goeth his way, and straightway forgetteth what manner of man he was. But whoso looketh into the perfect law of liberty, and continueth therein, he being not a forgetful hearer, but a doer of the work, this man shall be blessed in his deed.

GREEK WORDS
1. "doers" — ϖ (*poieo*): to do; to do creatively; to perform; the root for the word "poet"
2. "hearers only" — (*akroates*): used to describe individuals who audited a class rather than taking it for credit; hence, it depicted a hearer only, or one who had no intention of applying what he heard; he merely attended the class, but had no serious plans to implement what was taught

3. "deceiving" — ϖ   μ   (*paralogidzomai*): a miscalculation; a wrong analysis of facts or of a situation
4. "blessed" — μ   (*makarios*): blessed beyond measure

SYNOPSIS

Located in the city of Ephesus was the School of Tyrannus. This lecture hall was very close to where a synagogue once stood. Archaeologists suggest that the synagogue was replaced by the Celsus Library about 110 A.D. A careful look at the façade of the Celsus Library reveals the etching of a menorah that seems to corroborate this fact.

The apostle Paul taught in that synagogue for three months, and once he was finished there, he began teaching in the School of Tyrannus. He taught at that location for more than two years. God made him so effective in his efforts "that all they which dwelt in Asia heard the word of the Lord Jesus, both Jews and Greeks" (Acts 19:10). Although all who heard did not become Christians, all were clearly informed about Christ.

Paul knew people needed a solid, doctrinal foundation for their lives. Therefore, he taught them about the work of the Cross, the power of the resurrection, the anointing of the Holy Spirit, and the other fundamentals of the faith. We, too, need a strong foundation of faith in our lives. It is the strength of our foundation that will support us throughout our lifetime and determine our effectiveness to live for Christ.

The emphasis of this lesson:

To receive a clear appraisal of your spiritual level, you must continue to look at yourself in the "mirror" of the Word of God. It is the "perfect law of liberty" that brings freedom to those who do its precepts and are not hearers only.

You Are Called to Be a Doer of the Word and To Prosper in Christ

We are called to be "disciples" of Christ. In the Greek, "disciple" is the word *mathetes*, which is translated as a *committed student* or a *learner*. Jesus started out with 12 disciples. They were committed learners who didn't just *hear* what He said; they *did* what He said. Every time He taught His disciples something, He then sent them out to do it.

In the same way, you are called by God not just to be a *hearer* of His Word, but also to be a *doer*. Doing nothing results in nothing. If you want to reap great results in your life, it will require effort. Proverbs 28:19 says, "He that tilleth his land shall have plenty of bread: but he that followeth after vain persons shall have poverty enough."

Simply talking and dreaming about success will not produce it. Without being willing to get up and get to work, success will remain an elusive mirage in the distance that never becomes reality. The truth is, every teaching you hear, including the ten lessons in this study guide, are doable. You *can* take what you are hearing and begin to put it in to practice. Just start right where you are and ask the Holy Spirit to give you a supernatural *desire* to rise up in the midst of whatever situation you're in and begin to do what the Word says.

Hearer Versus *Doer*

As we noted in our previous lesson, James 1:22 says, "But be ye doers of the word, and not hearers only, deceiving your own selves." The word "doer" is the Greek word *poieo*, and it carries the idea of *creativity* or of *doing something creatively*. It is also the word where we get the word "poet." Basically, James said, "Don't just hear the Word of God; put it in to practice. If you can't conveniently find a way to do what the Word says, *get creative about it.*"

We are called to be doers of the Word and not hearers only. "Hearers only" is from the Greek word *akroates*, and it was used to describe *individuals who audited a class rather than taking it for credit.* They were students who were not as serious about what they were hearing and had little or no intention of applying what they heard. They merely attended the class, but had no real plans to implement what was taught. They were physically present, but mentally and emotionally, they could be "checked out." God doesn't want us to be *hearers only* of His Word, but rather *doers* of His Word.

The Scripture says those who are hearers only are in danger of "deceiving" themselves. "Deceiving" is from the Greek word *paralogidzomai*, which is a word librarians or scholars used to describe a *miscalculation*. In Greek culture, scholars would often put documents side by side to compare and analyze information. *Paralogidzomai* is the picture of a scholar who *made a miscalculation* or *came to the wrong conclusion* concerning his or her analysis of the facts.

In essence, James said, "If you think everything is going to turn out wonderfully just because you hear the Word, you have made a tragic miscalculation. It's not just *hearing* the Word that changes you. It's when you *do* God's Word that God's power is released."

The Hearer's Response to the Word

James continued in verse 23, saying, "For if any be a hearer of the word, and not a doer, he is like unto a man beholding his natural face in a glass." Those who are merely hearers of the Word are likened to a person who looked in a mirror. The word "glass" is actually the Greek word for a handheld mirror that could only be used to look at one small area at a time. This is a picture of the Holy Spirit, who deals with us step by step, one area at a time. Furthermore, the Greek here literally says, *"He looks at the face with which he was born."*

When most people get up in the morning and look in the mirror at the face they were born with, they see things about themselves they don't like — things they need to change. For example, their hair is a mess, their teeth need brushing, there are bags under their eyes, and the list goes on. How one responds to what he sees is the key to whether or not positive change is experienced.

Verse 24 says, "For he beholdeth himself, and goeth his way, and straightway forgetteth what manner of man he was." James says the *hearer only* quickly sees his flaws and knows what needs to be worked on — but rather than give attention to and deal with what's wrong, he goes on his way and forgets what he has seen. The Holy Spirit convicts him, but he quickly forgets about his conviction. The "hearer only" *may* have good intentions about doing what the Word says, but he doesn't take the time or put forth the effort needed to bring about change.

Those who are only hearers of the Word often view change as too difficult. After seeing what needs to change in their lives, they begin to delude themselves into thinking things are not as bad as they appear. Although they hear the Word, they don't stay in the Holy Spirit's presence long enough to allow Him to do the work only He can do. They won't let His truth really sink in and penetrate their heart.

The Doer's Response and the Hilarious Blessings That Result!

What happens when a *doer* looks into the Word? James 1:25 says, "But whoso looketh into the perfect law of liberty, and continueth therein, he being not a forgetful hearer, but a doer of the work, this man shall be blessed in his deed." The illustration of the mirror continues, only now the mirror has gone from a hand-held size to a much larger version.

The Greek in this verse indicates that once the doer sees something in his character that needs to change, he positions himself over a table-sized mirror so he can see and examine himself more fully. The doer really wants to do what is right and not just see his flaws and run from them. Out of concern for what has been revealed, he begins to hover over what the Bible calls "the perfect law of liberty," which is the Word of God.

To the *doer*, God's Word is the perfect law of liberty — not a law of bondage, but a law that produces freedom. He sees it and says to himself, *I will live by this Word and obey it fully. And if I am wrong in any area of my life, I will do whatever I need to do to adapt myself and get into agreement with the Word.*

The Greek word rendered "liberty" here is the same word used to describe *a slave who has been emancipated*. The doer understands that if he continues to look at himself in the mirror of God's Word — submitting to what it says and allowing it to be the law that governs his life — it will emancipate him, setting him free from all bondage.

In anticipation of transformation, the doer of the Word "continueth therein." This means he doesn't leave the mirror of God's Word until he sees what's wrong in his life made right. The result of his persistence is that he "shall be blessed in his deed." The word "deed" is the Greek word *ergon*, and it signifies that obedience to God's Word will not come easily; rather, it will require hard work. Nevertheless, if he *continues* in the Word, he will be "blessed" — the Greek word *makarios*, which means *hilariously blessed beyond measure*!

STUDY QUESTIONS

> Study to shew thyself approved unto God, a workman that needeth not to be ashamed, rightly dividing the word of truth.
> — 2 Timothy 2:15

1. Have you ever heard something from God's Word and struggled to believe you could actually do it? You're not alone. Thankfully, He has given us some encouraging promises to refute this lie of the enemy. Take a few moments to meditate on Deuteronomy 30:11-14. What is the Holy Spirit showing you in this passage? (Also consider Matthew 19:26, Mark 9:23, and Luke 1:37. Write out the verse that energizes you most.)

2. James 1:25 says if you *continue* in the Word of God, you will be *blessed beyond measure*! Continuing in the Word is the key. Read Second Timothy 3:14-17, Second Corinthians 3:12-18, and Jesus' words in John 8:31, 32. Describe the connection between *continuing* in the Word and *experiencing transformation*. (Also consider Joshua 1:8 and Psalm 1:1-6.)

PRACTICAL APPLICATION

> But be ye doers of the word, and not hearers only, deceiving your own selves.
> — James 1:22

1. Carefully review the descriptions of a *doer* of the Word and one who is a *hearer only*. Overall, which one best describes you? What evidence confirms this?

2. In what areas of your life are you more of a *hearer only*? Perhaps these are areas the Holy Spirit has already been bringing to your attention. Pause and pray, "Lord, why am I struggling to obey You in these areas? Please forgive me. Help me to do what You're instructing me to do, in Jesus' name." Be still and listen. What is the Holy Spirit saying to you?

www.ingramcontent.com/pod-product-compliance
Lightning Source LLC
Chambersburg PA
CBHW071414040426
42444CB00009B/2241